GENES & DISEASE

HEMOPHILIA

GENES & DISEASE

Alzheimer's Disease

Asthma

Cystic Fibrosis

Diabetes

Down Syndrome

Hemophilia

Huntington's Disease

Parkinson's Disease

Sickle Cell Disease

Tay-Sachs Disease

GENES & DISEASE

HEMOPHILIA

Michelle Raabe, Ph.D.

CHELSEA HOUSE
PUBLISHERS
An imprint of Infobase Publishing

Hemophilia

Chelsea House
An imprint of Infobase Publishing
132 West 31st Street
New York NY 10001

Library of Congress Cataloging-in-Publication Data

Raabe, Michelle.
  Hemophilia / Michelle Raabe.
      p. cm.—(Genes and disease)
  Includes bibliographical references and index.
  ISBN 978-0-7910-9648-2 (hardcover)
  1. Hemophilia—Popular works. 2. Blood coagulation disorders—
Popular works. I. Title. II. Series.

  RC642.R33 2008
  616.1'572—dc22   2008004897

You can find Chelsea House on the World Wide Web at
http://www.chelseahouse.com

Text design by Annie O'Donnell
Cover design by Ben Peterson

Printed in the United States of America

IBT NMSG 10 9 8 7 6 5 4 3 2

This book is printed on acid-free paper.

All links and Web addresses were checked and verified to be correct at the time of publication. Because of the dynamic nature of the Web, some addresses and links may have changed since publication and may no longer be valid.

CONTENTS

1 What Is Hemophilia? 7

2 The History of Hemophilia 25

3 The Inheritance of Hemophilia 40

4 Symptoms, Complications, and the
Diagnosis of Hemophilia 56

5 Treatment of Hemophilia: Whole-Blood
Transfusions to Clotting Factor Concentrates 70

6 Treatment of Hemophilia: Recombinant
Clotting Factors and Gene Therapy 83

7 Living with Hemophilia 98

Glossary 111

Bibliography 116

Further Reading 121

Picture Credits 125

Index 126

About the Author 133

1

WHAT IS HEMOPHILIA?

A FAMILY'S STORY

Jane and Kevin were about to have a baby, and it should have been the happiest time of their lives. Unfortunately, they had spent the last nine months nervous and worried. Jane and Kevin were afraid their baby would be born with a disease called **hemophilia**. Hemophilia is an inherited bleeding disorder that is passed from a mother to her son. The mutation that creates the disease hemophilia lies on an X-chromosome. Women have two X-chromosomes while men have an X- and a Y- chromosome. Jane's father had hemophilia, so when Jane was born, she inherited one X-chromosome from her mother, and from her father, she inherited the X-chromosome with the hemophilia gene. Women do not usually suffer the symptoms of the disease, so Jane has lived a healthy life. However, if she has a male child, he will receive one of her two X chromosomes and have a 50% chance of having hemophilia.

Jane and Kevin had the tests that told them they were having a boy. There are also tests that could tell them if an unborn child has hemophilia. These tests are very difficult to perform, very expensive, and not always accurate.

Because of these reasons, Jane and Kevin decided not to have the tests for hemophilia performed. As they waited for the arrival of their son, Jane and Kevin hoped for the best.

The big day came and Jane went into labor. It was a difficult birth. Not long after, it was apparent that the baby was having problems. His ankles were swelling up quickly, and they felt very hot to the touch. There was also a large lump forming on his head. The doctors diagnosed baby Joseph as having hemophilia.

The birthing process can cause bumps and bruises in normal babies, but these usually heal and fade away. In Joseph, however, the bleeding resulting from his small injuries would not stop because he was unable to clot his blood. Blood was filling up inside Joseph's joints and in the bump on his head, causing him to stay in the hospital for a long time, where he was given injections of the clotting factors that his body was not able to make on its own due to the disease that he had inherited. Over time, the clotting factors controlled his bleeding and the swellings went down.

The happy day came when Jane and Kevin were able to take their baby home. They were very excited, but they also had a lot on their minds. They knew that they would have to put extra padding in Joseph's crib, and probably cover their wood floors with soft carpeting. When Joseph begins to walk, they will have to decide whether he should wear a helmet, because brain bleeds are the most deadly injury a hemophiliac can have. There are many other questions they will have to think about: When Joseph is older, will he be able to play ball and other rough sports, or will he always have to sit on the sidelines? Will Joseph even attend regular school, or will he have to be tutored at home? Jane, Kevin, and Joseph have many decisions ahead of them.

THE BASICS

Hemophilia is an inherited bleeding disorder that mostly affects males. "Inherited" means that the disease is passed down through a family, and "bleeding disorder" means that hemophilia affects a person's blood. Specifically, the blood is missing important proteins that are necessary for the blood to clot. When a person's body is unable to clot blood correctly, the body has trouble stopping itself from bleeding. Hemophilia affects all kinds of people. A 2005 survey of 98 countries by the World Federation of Hemophilia estimated that more than 130,000 people in those countries have hemophilia.

There are actually two types of hemophilia, **hemophilia type A** and **hemophilia type B**. The first evidence that there may be two different forms of hemophilia was supplied in 1944 by a doctor in Argentina named Alfredo Pavlosky. He had samples of blood from two different hemophilic patients, and neither was able to clot. When Pavlosky mixed the two blood samples together, however, they clotted. This result seemed to indicate that each blood sample had something that the other was missing. This difference became clear in 1952 when three independent sets of researchers in San Francisco, New York, and Oxford described a "new hemophilia." Rosemary Biggs of the Oxford group called the newly discovered form of hemophilia "Christmas disease" because the first patient was Stephen Christmas and because the discovery was published in the Christmas edition of the British Medical Journal. Today, this form of hemophilia is more commonly referred to as type B hemophilia, and the earlier recognized form of the disease is called type A hemophilia. Hemophilia A is more common than hemophilia B. Type A hemophilia occurs once in every 20,000 births, while type B occurs once in every 60,000 births. Of all the people affected with hemophilia, 85% have type A and 15% have type B. There are also different levels of disease severity in hemophiliacs. People with severe forms of hemophilia experience spontaneous bleeding and bleeding into the joints and muscles, which can be quite painful. People with milder forms of hemophilia only experience bleeding episodes following an injury.

Clotting Factors

In the 1960s, the blood proteins called **clotting factors** were identified. There are a large number of clotting factors and they are numbered with roman numerals in the order that they were discovered. The clotting factors react with one another in a series of chemical reactions that stop bleeding by producing a blood clot. By understanding clotting factors, researchers where able to determine that people diagnosed with hemophilia type A are deficient in **factor VIII**, and people with hemophilia type B are deficient in **factor IX**. Factor VIII and factor IX are different structurally, and each plays a different role in producing a blood clot.

The Structure of Factor VIII and Factor IX

People with hemophilia A lack the clotting factor called factor VIII. The factor VIII protein is very large compared to other proteins, and it is made in liver cells. Before the factor VIII protein can be secreted into the bloodstream, it has to travel through the inside of the liver cell, where it is modified. Most importantly, the factor VIII protein is cut into three separate pieces: Two pieces are large and are called the heavy chains, and the third piece is small and is called the light chain. When the factor VIII protein leaves the liver cell and enters the bloodstream, these three protein sections remain loosely attached to each other. Because their attachment to one another is very weak, this makes the factor VIII protein unstable. Another protein called the **von Willebrand factor (vWF)** locks onto the factor VIII protein and helps to keep the heavy and light chains together. Even with a vWF attached, the factor VIII protein has a short half-life (the time it takes for half of the total amount of the protein to disappear from the blood) of 8 to 12 hours.

People with hemophilia type B are missing the clotting factor called factor IX. Compared to factor VIII, the factor IX protein is roughly five times smaller. Factor IX is also made in liver cells, but does not undergo many modifications and remains a single-chain protein. Because factor IX is a single protein chain, it is more stable than factor VIII. The stability of factor IX explains why it has a longer half-life (12 to 24 hours) than factor VIII. In addition, because factor IX stays in the bloodstream longer, at any given time there is usually more factor IX in the blood than factor VIII.

Hemophilia Is a Genetic Disease

Hemophilia is called a genetic disease because it is inherited from a parent. More specifically, boys inherit the disease from their mothers. The key to why hemophilia is a genetic disease lies in understanding that the flow of information in the human body begins with the body's genetic material, **deoxyribonucleic acid (DNA)**. In every cell of the human body, there is a fluid part called the cytoplasm and a separate section, called the nucleus, which is encased in a fatty membrane. The nucleus holds the cell's DNA. Chapter 3 will describe the structure and function of DNA in more detail, but for now, it is important to know that each DNA strand contains sections called **genes** that code for specific proteins. While DNA is located in the cell's nucleus, the actual proteins are made in the cytoplasm by structures called ribosomes. To get the information coded in a gene, which resides within the nucleus, to the ribosomes in the cytoplasm, the gene is copied into a piece of messenger ribonucleic acid (mRNA) in a process called **transcription**. The mRNA then crosses the nuclear membrane and enters the cytoplasm. Imagine mRNA as a set of instructions written on a piece of paper, which is then put into a bottle and floated out into the cytoplasm. Once in the cytoplasm, the mRNA finds a ribosome, and a protein is produced in a process called **translation**.

Diseases can occur if there is a change in the DNA code of a gene. Such a change is called a **mutation**. If the genetic code of the gene is incorrect, then the protein made from that gene will also be incorrect. In people with hemophilia, the genes that have become mutated are the ones that code for clotting factors VIII or IX. The severity of the gene mutation determines whether a nonfunctioning protein will be made, or whether no protein will be made at all. For both hemophilia A and B, the severity of the disease is related to the level of clotting-factor activity in the blood. Therefore, severe hemophiliacs may be unable to make any clotting factor VIII or IX at all, while a person with a milder form of the disease may be able to make some clotting factors, just ones that do not work well.

An interesting relationship has been observed between the size of the factor VIII gene and the frequency of hemophilia A. With 186,000 **nucleotides** (the subunits that make up a strand of DNA), the factor VIII gene is approximately 5.5 times larger than the factor IX gene (34,000 nucleotides). There are also 5.6 times more hemophilia A patients (85%) then hemophilia B patients (15%). Therefore, a logical reason for the connection would be that because the factor VIII gene is larger, it has more places for mutations to occur.

Hemophilia Is an X-Linked Genetic Disease

In the nucleus, the long and fragile strings of DNA take the form of **chromosomes**, which are protected from breaking

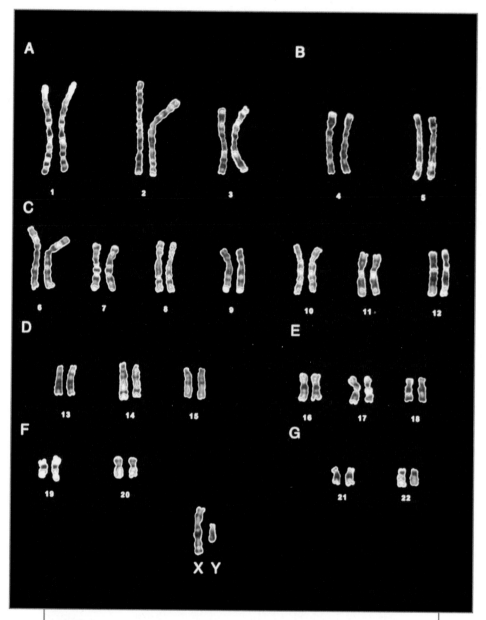

FIGURE 1.1   There are normally 23 pairs of chromosomes present in humans, and pair number 23 are the sex chromosomes. This figure shows a male's chromosomes: one X and one Y. A female has two X chromosomes. The diseases hemophilia A and B are called X-linked genetic diseases because it is the X chromosome that carries the genes for the clotting factors VIII and IX.

by being compact and tightly wound. The human body has 46 chromosomes. Two are designated the **sex chromosomes** because they determine the sex of a baby. Two X chromosomes (XX) determine that a baby will be female, while one X and one Y chromosome (XY) result in a male child. The other 44 chromosomes are called **autosomal chromosomes**.

When a gene is located on either the X or Y chromosome, it is said to be a sex-linked trait. Both hemophilia *A* and hemophilia B are categorized as X-linked genetic diseases because the genes for factor VIII and factor IX are located on the X chromosome. The sex linkage of hemophilia is important in understanding why women are carriers of the disease, although it is usually men who experience symptoms of the disease. Women have two X chromosomes, so if one contains a hemophilic mutation, the other normal X chromosome can still supply the factor VIII or IX proteins. These women are called carriers because they carry a mutation for hemophilia, which can be passed down to one of their children. Men have only one X chromosome, so if it contains a hemophilic mutation, their ability to generate working clotting factors is diminished or eliminated. In only very rare instances would a women inherit a mutated X chromosome from both her mother and father, and therefore express the disease hemophilia.

It is important to note that although hemophilia A and B are categorized as hereditary diseases, in approximately 30% of cases an individual is said to have experienced a **spontaneous mutation**, a brand new mutation that just appeared in one of their clotting-factor genes rather than being inherited. Most of the time, this diagnosis is made because there is no family history of hemophilia. However, this category also includes cases where there is a family history, but one that remains unidentified. For example, maybe for generations only girls were born. That would allow the hemophilic trait to go unnoticed for a long time.

Another example might be a person who is adopted and has no knowledge of his or her birth parents.

HEMOSTASIS

In the word **hemostasis**, "hemo" means blood, and "stasis" means to stop. Hemostasis thus describes how the body is able to stop the flow of blood after an injury. The process of hemostasis begins about 20 seconds after an injury and is similar in all mammals. The clotting of blood, or

THE ROLE OF VITAMIN K

Vitamin K is needed for the production of clotting factors. The K in vitamin K stands for "koagulation," the German form of the word coagulation, because the first scientific reports of this vitamin were made in Germany. We get some vitamin K from foods such as spinach, lettuce, cabbage, broccoli, cereals, meat, and cow's milk. A lot of our vitamin K, however, is made by bacteria, mostly *Escherichia coli*, that live in our large intestines. The resident bacteria in our large intestines are an example of what is called our normal flora. Our normal flora consists of the bacteria that live throughout our bodies but cause us no harm. In fact, our normal flora protects us from microbes that are more dangerous and further helps us by making things like vitamins. Our normal flora is very important to our health, and we are not talking about just a few microbes. We have 1×10^{13} cells that make up our bodies. We also have 1×10^{14} bacterial cells that live on and in our bodies. When babies are born, they have not had time to develop their normal flora, which is why newborns have to receive vitamin K drops in their eyes. It is through exposure to the environment, mainly putting things in their mouths, that babies establish their normal flora.

coagulation, is an important part of hemostasis. Efficient coagulation requires a number of ingredients: **platelets** (small blood cells that help clot blood); a healthy liver (the clotting factors are made by the liver); vitamin K

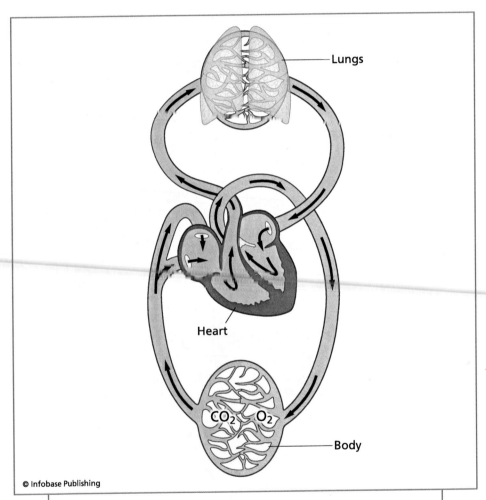

FIGURE 1.2 This is a diagram of the human circulatory system. The blue vessels show blood that is returning from the body, depleted of oxygen. The red vessels show blood that has picked up oxygen from the lungs. The arrows indicate the direction of the blood's movement.

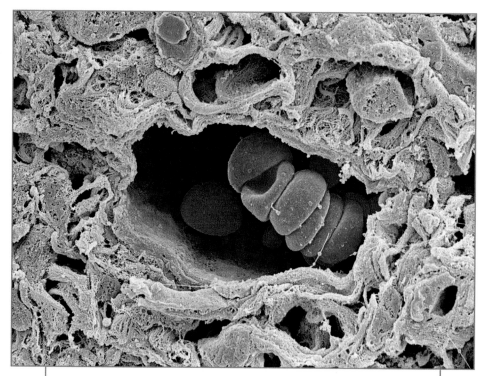

FIGURE 1.3   This photo shows the cross-section of a blood vessel. There are three main cell layers: the outermost layer, consisting of collagen and elastin; a middle layer, which consists of muscle; and the innermost layer, composed of endothelial cells (endothelium).

(necessary to maintain a healthy liver); and calcium (a mineral needed by the body to perform chemical reactions). Hemostasis is divided into two phases: primary hemostasis, which involves the injured blood vessel and platelet cells; and secondary hemostasis, which involves the clotting factors.

Primary Hemostasis

The blood vessels play a key role in primary hemostasis. Blood vessels are tubes that enable the blood to travel throughout the body. Arteries are blood vessels that carry blood away from the heart, and veins are blood vessels that carry blood back to the heart. As the blood moves through the vessels, it absorbs nutrients and water from the intestines and oxygen from the lungs and delivers these to the cells of the body. The blood also absorbs the waste products of the cells and carries these away to be filtered by the liver and kidneys.

Blood vessels are made up of three layers of cells. The outermost layer contains elastin and collagen fibers. Collagen fibers are long, tough proteins that give this layer support and strength, and elastin fibers are elastic and allow the blood vessels to stretch. The middle layer is thick muscle tissue, which contracts and relaxes the blood vessel to control the flow of blood. The innermost layer is the endothelium, which is a single layer of endothelial cells that line the interior surface of the blood vessel.

Primary hemostasis begins with an injury to the blood vessel that is severe enough to damage the endothelium. Chemical signals released from the damaged endothelial cells help launch the process of hemostasis by signaling the body that an injury has occurred and that coagulation needs to begin. The blood vessel's thick middle layer of muscle cells contracts to slow the flow and loss of blood. Next, the blood vessel's outer cell layer plays its role. The collagen fibers within this outer layer are covered with von Willebrand factor (vWF) proteins. When platelets in the escaping blood encounter these proteins, they become activated. The activated platelets now release chemical signals that bring in additional platelets to the injured area. All of these activated platelets begin to change shape, become very sticky, and clump together. All combined, the result of primary hemostasis is the formation of a **platelet plug** that stops up the hole in the torn blood vessel.

Secondary Hemostasis

The platelet plug formed in primary hemostasis is able to seal the hole in the blood vessel only temporarily. It is not strong enough to hold together very long, which is why the second phase of hemostasis is important. Secondary hemostasis involves a complex set of chemical reactions involving the many different clotting factors, with the result being the production of fibrin. Fibrin is a long, thick, strong protein that is inserted into and around the platelet plug to strengthen it. The platelet plug now becomes a **fibrin clot**. The newly established fibrin clot is strong enough to hold the damaged blood vessel together while the different cell layers repair themselves.

The chemical reactions in secondary hemostasis can be divided into three pathways: the extrinsic (tissue factor pathway), the intrinsic (contact actuation pathway), and the common. We can envision their actions as a capital Y. The left arm of the Y is the extrinsic pathway and is responsible for beginning the reactions of secondary hemostasis. The extrinsic pathway is not disrupted in a person with hemophilia. The right arm of the Y is the intrinsic pathway, which acts to strengthen the clotting process once it has been started by the extrinsic pathway. It is the intrinsic pathway that is damaged in a person with hemophilia. The extrinsic and intrinsic pathways lead to the common pathway of reactions, which is represented by the lower body of the Y. It is important to understand that a person needs all of the clotting factors, each performing their assigned reaction, each in the proper order, for a stable fibrin clot to form.

In 1955, it was decided that all of the clotting factors would be designated by roman numerals and that they would be numbered in the order in which they were discovered. For the discussion of hemophilia, we will concentrate on the

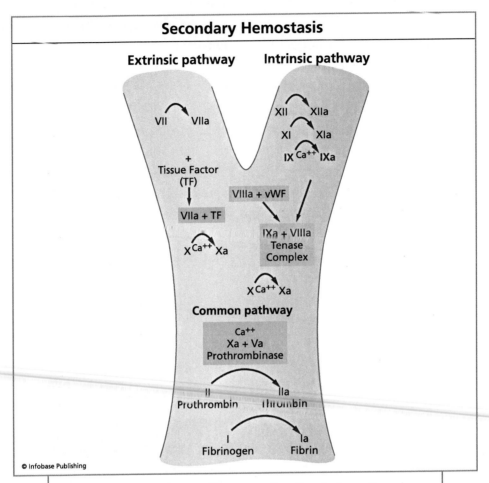

Secondary Hemostasis

Extrinsic pathway   Intrinsic pathway

VII   VIIa

XII   XIIa

XI   XIa

IX Ca++ IXa

+
Tissue Factor
(TF)

VIIIa + vWF

VIIa + TF

X Ca++ Xa

IXa + VIIIa
Tenase
Complex

X Ca++ Xa

Common pathway

Ca++
Xa + Va
Prothrombinase

II   IIa
Prothrombin   Thrombin

I   Ia
Fibrinogen   Fibrin

© Infobase Publishing

FIGURE 1.4   This diagram illustrates the chemical reactions in secondary hemostasis. The extrinsic pathway (left) begins clotting while the intrinsic pathway (right) strengthens the process. The intrinsic pathway is defective in hemophiliacs. Factor VIII (blue) is missing in people with hemophilia A, and factor IX (red) is missing in people with hemophilia B.

intrinsic pathway because it contains the clotting factors that are missing in hemophiliacs (factor VIII and IX). In the intrinsic pathway, the clotting factors XII, XI, X, IX, II, and I are **enzymes**, proteins that drive a specific chemical reaction. These enzymes act to cut other proteins into smaller pieces. The clotting factors V and VIII are not enzymes; they are called cofactors, which are substances needed by enzymes to make the chemical reactions occur.

The chemical reactions of secondary hemostasis have to occur in a specific order because each reaction creates the enzyme that will carry out the next reaction. More specifically, the chemical reactions of secondary hemostasis work like this. Think of the clotting factors XII, XI, X, IX, II, and I as scissors. To control when and what they cut, they are kept in inactive forms. Imagine the inactive clotting factors as scissors with rubber bands wrapped around the blades so that they cannot cut. The only way to activate an inactive clotting factor is to cut the rubber band. For example, activated clotting factor A-active, which was activated in a previous chemical reaction, cuts the rubber band of clotting factor B, thus activating it. Then, the newly activated clotting factor B-active will go on to activate clotting factor C, and so on. The clotting factors V and VIII are not enzymes because they do not cut other proteins. They are cofactors, or "enzyme helpers." Cofactors are allowed to circulate in the bloodstream in their active forms.

In the following discussion of the intrinsic and common pathways, all of the clotting factors are designated by roman numerals, and a small "a" following the number indicates the active form of the factor.

1. In the intrinsic pathway, the very first chemical reaction occurs on the collagen surface of the injured blood vessel. Factor XII is converted to the active form, factor XIIa.
2. Factor XIIa converts factor XI to factor XIa.
3. Factor XIa converts factor IX to factor IXa. Calcium is needed for this reaction.
4. Cofactor VIII circulates in the bloodstream in an active form (factor VIIIa), and it circulates bound

to another protein called the von Willebrand factor (vWF). The vWF helps to stabilize the activated form of factor VIIIa.

5. The factor VIIIa–vWF complex binds to factor IXa, the vWF is released, and the IXa + VIIIa combination is called the tenase complex. Calcium is needed for this reaction.

6. The tenase complex converts factor X to factor Xa. Calcium is needed for this reaction.

In addition to the intrincic pathway, the extrinsic pathway also produces activated factor Xa, although by a different means. It is factor Xa that begins the common pathway of secondary hemostasis.

7. Factor Xa binds to factor Va, and this complex is called prothrombinase. Calcium is needed for this reaction to occur. Just like factor VIII, factor V is a cofactor and circulates in the blood in its active form.

8. Prothrombinase (Xa–Va) then converts factor II (prothrombin) to factor IIa (thrombin).

9. Factor IIa converts factor I (fibrinogen) to factor Ia (fibrin).

10. As the fibrin molecules accumulate, they collect in and around the platelet plug to glue it together. More specifically, the fibrin molecules are said to "cross-link" the platelet cells.

11. A fibrin clot has now been formed.

TWO BLEEDING DISORDERS THAT ARE NOT HEMOPHILIA

Hemophilia type A and hemophilia type B are considered the only true hemophilia diseases. However, two other bleeding disorders used to be confused with hemophilia, factor XI deficiency, and von Willebrand disease.

The bleeding disorder called factor XI deficiency used to be called hemophilia C. A lack of functioning clotting factor XI causes this disease, which affects about one out of every 100,000 people in the U.S. One of the reasons factor XI deficiency was mistaken as hemophilia was because factor XI is part of the intrinsic pathway, just like factors VIII and IX. However, factor XI deficiency is different from hemophilia A and B because it is an autosomal hereditary disease. This means that the factor XI gene is not located on one of the sex chromosomes, but instead lies on one of the 44 autosomal chromosomes. Specifically, the gene for factor XI is located on chromosome number 4.

Because factor XI deficiency is autosomal, it affects both men and women equally. Factor XI deficiency also appears to be most common in Jewish people of Ashkenazi descent. Of all the people affected by this disease, half do not have a bleeding problem and half do. Of the half that does have bleeding problems, they can range from mild to severe, but not usually as severe as hemophilia A or B. Also different from hemophilia A and B, the degree of bleeding experienced as a result of deficiencies in factor XI are not related to levels of factor XI activity in the blood.

Von Willebrand disease (vWD) is the most common hereditary bleeding disorder in humans, but it is not a form of hemophilia. Von Willebrand disease is named after Erik Adolf von Willebrand, who first described the disease in 1926. The disease is caused by a deficiency in von Willebrand factor (vWF), the blood protein that activates platelets and circulates in the blood holding the three VIIIa protein fragments together. Deficiencies in factor VIII are observed in both hemophilia A and vWD, which is why the difference between the two diseases was confusing until it was demonstrated that vWF and factor VIII were two separate proteins.

Unlike hemophilia A and B, von Willebrand disease is autosomal: The location of the vWF gene is on chromosome number 12, and it affects both men and women. There are three types of vWD. Type 1 is the most mild and type 3 is the most severe. Some patients with type 3 vWD can experience severe disease symptoms, including bleeding into the joints.

2

THE HISTORY
OF HEMOPHILIA

THE ANCIENT HISTORY OF HEMOPHILIA:
HEMOPHILIA IN THE TALMUD

Hemophilia is an ancient disease. The first written reference to a bleeding disorder, very likely hemophilia, was in the Babylonian Talmud 1,500 years ago. The Talmud is a written record of discussions between great Jewish scholars, in which they documented their opinions on law, ethics, customs, and history. The Talmud is divided into six major sections, and each section is further divided into books. The section Nashim and the book Yebamoth include references to severe bleeding, and even death, after circumcision. Circumcision is a procedure in which the foreskin, the skin that covers the tip of the penis, is cut away. Circumcision is usually performed when a boy is just a baby, so if the boy is a hemophiliac, it can be the first time a bleeding episode occurs. In the Talmud, the Jewish scholars not only recognized a bleeding disorder in some boys, but also suspected the bleeding disorder to be inherited.

In the case of circumcision, one can well understand why the operation is dangerous with some children and not with others. Since the members of one family may bleed profusely [a lot], while those of another family may bleed little. (Nashim, Yebamoth, 64b)

The following section of the Talmud demonstrates two points. First, because circumcision is very important in the Jewish religion, to excuse boys from this procedure showed that Jewish scholars recognized the seriousness of a bleeding disorder. Second, because only relationships to the mother are discussed suggests that the scholars suspected the disease was inherited through the mother's side of the family.

For it was taught: if she circumcised her first child and he died, and a second one also died, she must not circumcise her third child. (Rabbi Judah the Patriarch-Nashim, Yebamoth, 64b)

Further evidence for the authors suspecting the disorder was inherited through the woman's side of the family is offered in another section of the book of Yebamoth. This passage tells the story of three sisters whose sons had died after circumcision, so Rabbi Simeon ben Gamiliel excused the fourth sister from having to circumcise her son.

It once happened with four sisters at Sepphoris that when the first had circumcised her child he died; when the second circumcised her child, he also died, and when the third circumcised her child he also died. The fourth came before Rabbi Simeon b. Gamaliel who told her, "You must not circumcise the child." (Nashim, Yebamoth, 64b)

Albucasis
Abul Qasim Khalaf ibn al-Abbas al-Zahravi is his full name, Abu Qasim Al-Zahravi for short, and Albucasis is the west-

ern name given to a great physician who lived in the middle ages. Albucasis was a Spanish-born Muslim who became one of the most well-known physicians in history. He wrote a 30-volume medical encyclopedia called *Al-Tasrif* (*The Method of Medicine*) that was used to teach medical students all over the world for centuries. In this encyclopedia, Albucasis wrote the first accurate description of a bleeding disorder that was transmitted by seemingly healthy mothers to their sons.

In *Al-Tasrif*, Albucasis also described the earliest treatment for hemophilia when he wrote that cautery could be used to control bleeding in these and other injured people. Cautery is a procedure in which metal tools are heated in a fire until they glow bright red and then are placed on the body for a few seconds. The intense heat helps to coagulate the blood and to kill microbes that may cause infection. While the method can result in a lot of tissue damage from the burn, it is a quick and easy way to stop bleeding (although painful for the patient), so it was a procedure long used on battlefields.

The Family Tree of Hemophilia in America

After Albucasis's writings, references to hemophilia were rare until 1803. Dr. John C. Otto, a well-respected doctor in the Philadelphia area, was born in New Jersey to both a father and a grandfather who were doctors. Otto is famous for having traced the disease of hemophilia through three generations of a family to a single woman named Smith, who settled near Plymouth, New Hampshire, between 1727 to 1737. Otto published his research under the title, *An Account of an Hemorrhagic Disposition Existing in Certain Families.* Not only was it the first family study to be published in America, it is also one of the earliest accurate clinical descriptions of hemophilia. One of the most important points that Otto

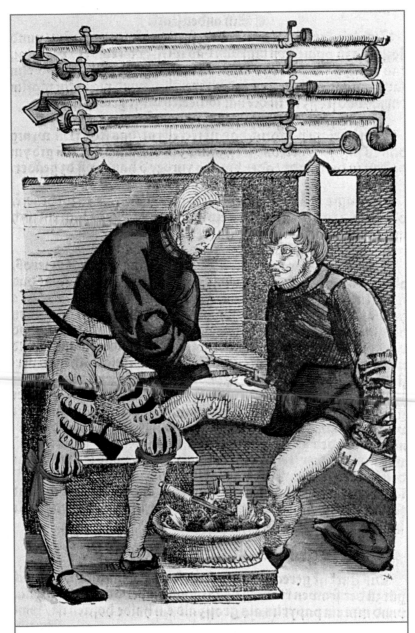

FIGURE 2.1 In this engraving from the sixteenth century, a physician is applying a piece of metal that has been heated in a fire until it is red hot to a man's wound. The hot metal will burn the injured tissues causing some cell damage, but will also seal the open wound and stop any bleeding.

made in his publication was to outline what became the three distinguishing features of hemophilia: an *inherited* disease that causes *bleeding* in *males*.

While Otto's paper on Mrs. Smith's family was a huge achievement in educating people about the inheritance of hemophilia, it really was only the tip of the iceberg. It is believed that Mrs. Smith was part of the large Appleton-Swain family of Reading, Massachusetts. The Appleton family has been studied by a number of researchers, and an enormous family tree of hemophilia covering 400 years and 13 generations has been constructed, showing 27 known hemophiliacs and 25 proven carriers.

It is important to understand that while the disease hemophilia has been long known, it was not until the early 1820s that it was actually given the name "hemophilia" by a German scientist named Johann Lukas Schönlein. This name then became official when one of Schönlein's students, Frederick Hopff, published the term in 1828.

THE ROYAL DISEASE

Hemophilia is often referred to as "the royal disease." Hemophilia presented itself in the royal families of Britain, Germany, Spain, and Russia, beginning with Queen Victoria of England (1819–1901). Queen Victoria passed the mutation to her son Leopold and to several of her daughters, who married into royal families across the continent. Because neither of her parents had family histories of hemophilia, nor did her husband Prince Albert, it is likely Queen Victoria experienced a spontaneous mutation.

Victoria had four sons, but it was her eighth child and youngest son, Leopold, who had hemophilia. Leopold led a very restricted life as his mother attempted to confine and protect him from injury. In an effort to escape his

FIGURE 2.2   Queen Victoria was queen of Great Britain from 1837 until her death in 1901. Queen Victoria is thought to have experienced a spontaneous mutation that made her a carrier of the disease hemophilia.

mother, Leopold married and lived long enough to have two children, a son who was normal and a daughter who was a carrier of hemophilia. Most likely, because Leopold was a wealthy man who did not have to perform hard manual labor for a living, he managed to live a relatively long life for

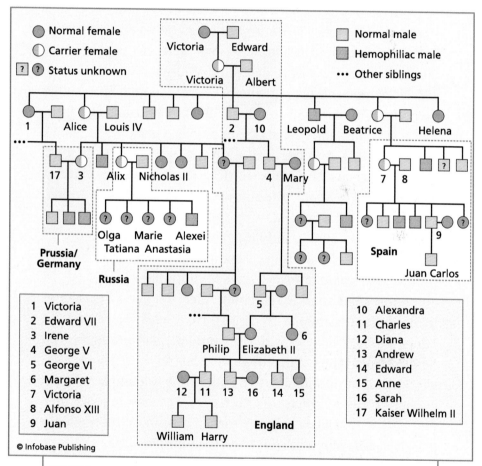

FIGURE 2.3 This genealogy outlines the path of hemophilia throughout the royal families of Europe. The disease began with Queen Victoria, and because there was no family history prior to her children, it is thought she experienced a spontaneous mutation. Victoria's daughters were carriers of the disease and brought it into the royal houses of Germany (Prussia), Russia, and Spain.

a nineteenth-century hemophiliac; he died at the age of 30 after a minor fall. As for the current royal family of England, they descended from Victoria's eldest son, Edward the VII, who was not a hemophiliac. Of her nine children, Victoria also had two daughters that we now know were carriers of hemophilia. Victoria's youngest daughter, Beatrice, was a shy girl who stayed with her mother even after marrying her husband, Henry of Battenburg. It is believed that two of her three sons had hemophilia, but none of the three had children. Beatrice's only daughter, Victoria Eugenie, was a carrier of hemophilia, and she became Queen of Spain after marrying Alfonso XIII in 1906. Eugenie had six children, and two of her sons were hemophiliacs. Because Eugenie's husband, King Alfonso, was a tyrant, a revolution in 1931 drove the royals into exile. In 1975, however, the monarchy was restored in Spain with Alfonso's grandson, Juan Carlos, being crowned king. Juan Carlos's father, Don Juan, is the youngest of Alfonso's and Eugenie's four sons, and is one of the two who did not inherit hemophilia. Therefore, the current King of Spain does not have hemophilia.

Victoria had another daughter, Alice, who was a carrier of hemophilia and who married into the German royal family. Of her two sons, Frederick was a hemophiliac. At the age of three he died from internal bleeding after falling through an open window. Of her remaining five children, two daughters were carriers of hemophilia. Alice's daughter Irene married her first cousin, Prince Henry of Prussia. In spite of their efforts to hide it, two of Irene's sons were hemophiliacs. Alice's other carrier daughter, Alexandra, carried the disease to the royal family of Russia when she married Czar Nikolai Romanov II.

The story of Alexandra and Nikolai is most memorable because they were the last of the Russian royals. Czarina Alexandra bore four daughters and one son, Alexei, who was a hemophiliac. In a desperate effort to ensure the safety of their only heir, Alexandra and Nikolai turned to a charismatic monk known as Rasputin. Rasputin had great success at using hypnosis to control young Alexei's bleeding episodes and in relieving his chronic joint pain. Because of his ability to help the Russian prince, Rasputin gained great

FIGURE 2.4 This photograph of the Romanov royal family was taken in 1913. Standing are the daughters Tatiana and Olga. On the arm of her mother's chair is the daughter Marie. The Czarina Alexandra and Czar Nikolai are in the center of the photograph. Sitting on the floor is the only son Alexei, and seated on the far right is his sister Anastasia.

HYPNOSIS AND HEMOPHILIA

Surprisingly, the most effective treatment that Rasputin used to relieve Alexei's pain was hypnosis. The use of hypnosis not only relieved his chronic pain, but also may have helped control the young boy's hemorrhages. Today, hypnosis is still available to hemophiliacs for controlling their bleeding episodes. Hypnosis is defined as a state of very deep concentration and focused attention. In simple terms, a patient is given mental images to think about when they are experiencing a bleed, for example, imagining a switch at the site of the bleed that could turn off the flow of blood. Detailed and scientifically accepted studies on the link between hypnosis and hemophilia have just recently begun. For years, however, evidence has accumulated that suggests that patients who learn self-hypnosis experience fewer and less severe bleeding episodes, and have greater success at controlling bleeding episodes with less clotting factor. In addition to controlling bleeding, the benefits of hypnosis to hemophiliacs include increased feelings of confidence and the improved ability to reduce stress, which has also been linked to having a healthy immune system.

influence with the royal family, and his political powers grew enormously. By 1916, many of the country's aristocrats (the wealthy social class) and government officials were fed up with having to bow down to this nobody they called the "mad monk." In spite of the Czar and Czarina's favor towards Rasputin, a group invited him to dinner and attempted to kill him with poisoned wine, but he lived. The group then shot him, but he lived. Finally, the assassins threw Rasputin into the river where he finally died. Alexandra and Nikolai were devastated, and Alexandra was often seen crying over

Rasputin's grave. However, in 1917, revolution broke out, and Nikolai, Alexandra, and their five children were brutally executed.

HEPATITIS AND HIV IN HEMOPHILIACS

By the 1970s, replacement treatments for hemophilia had evolved to using clotting factors that were concentrated from human blood. These factor VIII and IX supplies were mass-produced by combining the donated blood of thousands of people. Unfortunately, some of these donors carried a dangerous virus in their blood called **hepatitis C**. Many things can cause the disease hepatitis, but the **hepatitis C virus (HCV)** specifically causes the disease called hepatitis C. HCV is spread by blood-to-blood contact with an infected person. The virus contains a single strand of **RNA** enclosed in a protein capsule that is covered in a membrane, called an envelope. The virus enters a liver cell, uses the cell's own enzymes and ribosomes to make new virus particles, and the new particles bud from the cell. Viruses bud by pushing up against the inside of the cell and eventually forcing their way through to the outside. As they emerge from the cell, they wrap themselves in a piece of the liver cell's outer membrane, thus coating themselves in envelopes. Over time, because the liver cell was made a slave to the virus and was not able to make the things it needed to survive, the cell eventually dies. Hepatitis C is a chronic disease, which means that there is no cure; an infected person has the virus in his or her blood the rest of his or her life.

The amazing thing was that in the 1970's, it was no secret that the clotting factor medicines were contaminated with HCV. It is important to understand that at this time, the disease hepatitis C was not well understood; it was thought to be just a mild viral infection. Because the number one

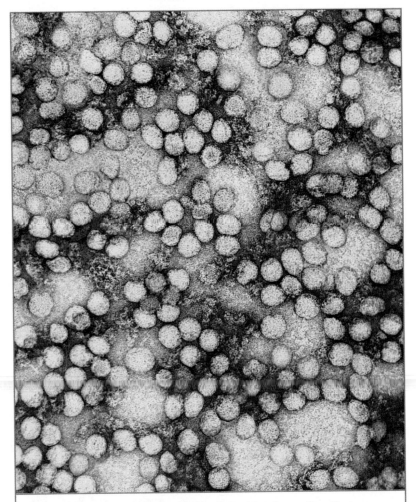

FIGURE 2.5 In the 1970s, much of the blood supplies that were used to treat people with hemophilia were infected with the hepatities C virus (HCV), pictured here. HCV causes a life-long infection that eventually destroys the liver. Today, blood supplies are screened and treated to prevent transmission during blood transfusions.

cause of death in hemophiliacs at that time was uncontrolled bleeding, and not hepatitis-related liver disease, the benefits of using hepatitis-contaminated blood outweighed the risks.

The reason that hepatitis was thought to be only a mild infection was because it has a very long incubation period, the time between when the body becomes infected and when symptoms first appear. With hepatitis C, few people have symptoms until 20 years after being infected with HCV. When the disease does present itself, it is very slow to progress. It was not until the mid-1980s that doctors began to realize that hepatitis C was not a mild infection, but was in fact deadly. Even then, blood supplies continued to be contaminated with HCV because a reliable blood test to identify infected blood donors was not available until the 1990s.

The hemophilic community was hit hard by the hepatitis epidemic. Today, it is estimated that 44% of all hemophiliacs have the hepatitis C virus. Because the liver manufactures the body's clotting factors, hepatitis is particularly dangerous to hemophiliacs. As liver functioning decreases because of a hepatitis infection, a person with mild or moderate hemophilia can progress to severe hemophilia.

In the mid-1980s, the severity of the hepatitis infections became clear. Because tests to separate infected and uninfected blood were not available, methods were developed to kill viruses in the donated blood supplies. Today in the U.S. there are four methods used to inactivate viruses in blood-derived products: (1) heat treatment of the product when it is a liquid (pasteurization); (2) heat treatment after the product has been freeze-dried; (3) adding detergents to break open and kill the viruses; and (4) the use of **immunoaffinity purification methods**. The latter method uses antibodies to separate the factor VIII and IX proteins away from other blood proteins and contaminating viruses. While some companies use one method and others use a combination, current factor VIII and IX products are monitored by the Food and Drug Administration (FDA) and are considered safe.

It was fortunate that these viral inactivation methods were developed to reduce hepatitis infections, because in

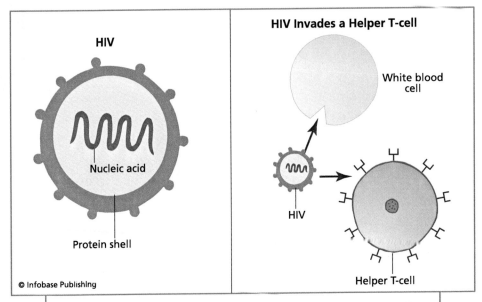

FIGURE 2.6 HIV attacks certain white blood cells. The RNA of HIV will be copied into the DNA of the infected white blood cell.

the early 1980s, the hemophilia community was hit with a second blood-borne virus, the **human immunodeficiency virus (HIV)**. HIV is the virus that causes acquired immunodeficiency disease or AIDS. The HIV epidemic officially began in 1981 with the recognition of an unusual type of cancer in men. Very quickly, in 1982, it was discovered that HIV can be transmitted through blood, and the first case of HIV in a hemophiliac patient was reported. As with hepatitis, people who did not know they were HIV positive donated blood that was then used to make clotting factor medicines. Statistics from the National Hemophilic Foundation estimate that from the late 1970s to the mid-1980s, nearly half of all hemophiliacs became HIV positive, with 80% of severe hemophiliacs becoming infected. Sadly, many of these infected hemophiliacs were children.

HIV and HCV are both enveloped viruses that contain RNA. HCV, however, contains one strand of RNA while HIV contains two strands of RNA. Furthermore, the manner in which these viruses make proteins is also different. HCV enters a cell and produces proteins directly from its one strand of RNA. HIV is classified as a retrovirus, which means that once it is inside the target cell, special enzymes called reverse transcriptase copy its RNA into DNA. The copies of viral DNA take over the host cell by inserting themselves into the cell's DNA. From where it sits inside the host's DNA, HIV uses the cell to make new viruses that bud and get their envelope from the host cell's outer membrane. Like HCV, HIV is a life-long chronic infection and has no cure. Different from HCV, HIV targets cells of the immune system, the body's system of defenses against disease and infection, and particularly the cells called T cells.

HIV is also similar to HCV in that it has a long incubation period. When first infected, a person experiences flu-like symptoms, but then for the next 10 years or more, the person could have no signs of having HIV. It can also be difficult to detect people who were recently infected with HIV because antibodies to the virus can take up to six months to appear in the bloodstream. Because the virus targets and kills cells of the immune system, the infected person's immune system grows continually weaker with time until they eventually enter the AIDS stage of the disease. The diagnosis of AIDS comes when a person's T cell count drops below 200 per milliliter of blood and experiences the symptoms of AIDS, which include severe fatigue, weight loss, fevers, swollen glands, and night sweats. Death usually comes from infection with common bacteria, yeast, parasites, and viruses that ordinarily do not cause serious disease in people with a healthy immune system.

Today, with the application of virus-inactivating methods, factor VIII and IX treatments are very safe. However, there is always the risk of emerging diseases—diseases that are brand new, like hepatitis C and HIV were 40 years ago.

THE INHERITANCE
OF HEMOPHILIA

THE CELL

The cell is the basic unit of life. All cells may be classified into two fundamental types: prokaryotes and eukaryotes. Prokaryotic cells lack a nucleus and other membrane-bound organelles. Eukaryotic cells are more complex and larger than prokaryotic cells. Most importantly, in a eukaryotic cell the DNA is contained in the nucleus, which is surrounded by a membrane. As noted in Chapter 2, the nucleus acts as the command center of the cell, because DNA holds all the information that the cell needs to perform its functions.

DNA

All living organisms have DNA as their genetic material. In 1962, James Watson, Francis Crick, and Maurice Wilkins won the Nobel Prize in medicine because they analyzed the structure of DNA in the early 1950's. They found that each DNA molecule is made of two strands held together by chemical bonds, and that the strands twist around each other like a long winding staircase. They called this structure a double helix.

Each strand of DNA is made up of smaller units called nucleotides. Each nucleotide has three parts: a sugar

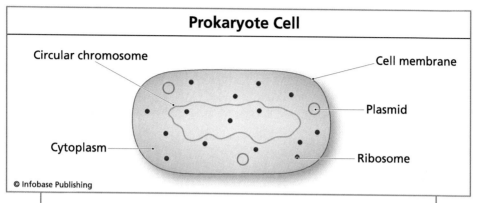

Prokaryote Cell

Circular chromosome

Cell membrane

Plasmid

Cytoplasm

Ribosome

© Infobase Publishing

FIGURES 3.1 & 3.2   These illustrations show the differences between prokaryote and eukaryote cells. Eukaryotic cells are usually much larger than prokaryotic cells. Eukaryotic cells also have membrane-bound organelles and a membrane-bound nucleus. Prokaryotic cells lack both of these.

(deoxyribose), a phosphate group, and a carbon ring that contains nitrogen molecules (a nitrogenous base). Each strand of the DNA's double helix is made by the phosphate of one nucleotide attaching to the sugar of the nucleotide above it. This is why DNA is said to have a sugar-phosphate backbone. Two strands of DNA attach to each other through the bases to make a double-stranded DNA molecule. The bases always pair in the same way: adenine (A) to thymine (T) and guanine (G) to cytosine (C), except in RNA, where adenine pairs with uracil (U).

From Genes to Proteins

Information in every cell flows in one direction, from genes to proteins, and two processes help this information to be passed along: transcription and translation.

Transcription

Transcription only takes place in the cell's nucleus and is the first step on the road to producing a protein. Transcription

Eukaryote Cell

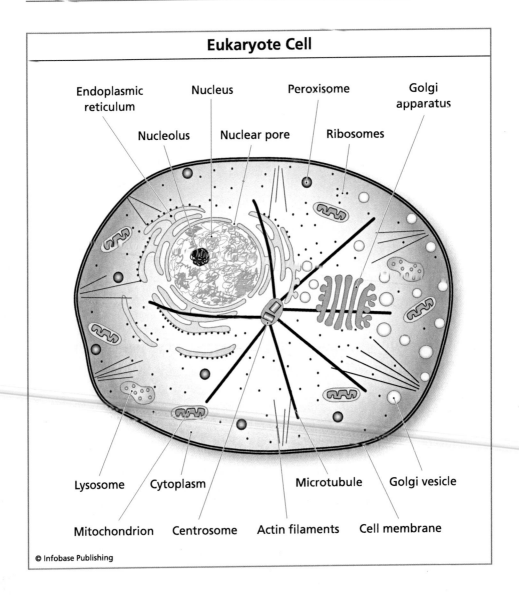

Endoplasmic reticulum · Nucleus · Peroxisome · Golgi apparatus

Nucleolus · Nuclear pore · Ribosomes

Lysosome · Cytoplasm · Microtubule · Golgi vesicle

Mitochondrion · Centrosome · Actin filaments · Cell membrane

© Infobase Publishing

is the process by which the DNA code of a gene is copied into a special type of RNA called messenger RNA (mRNA). Messenger RNA acts as a messenger by transporting coded information for specific proteins from the nucleus to the parts of the cytoplasm where proteins are produced.

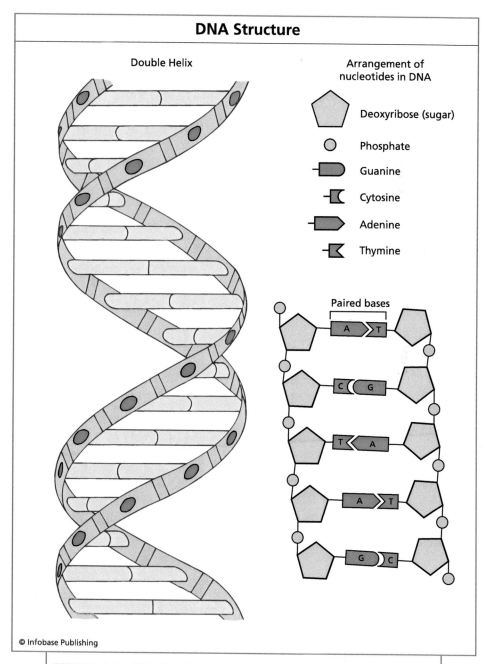

DNA Structure

Double Helix

Arrangement of nucleotides in DNA

Deoxyribose (sugar)

Phosphate

Guanine

Cytosine

Adenine

Thymine

Paired bases

A T

C G

T A

A T

G C

© Infobase Publishing

FIGURE 3.3 This drawing shows the basic structure of DNA and the base pairs that make up the double helix.

At the beginning of transcription, an enzyme called RNA polymerase recognizes a special DNA "start signal" called a promoter. The enzyme settles on the promoter like a train on a railroad track. The attachment of the RNA polymerase causes the double-stranded DNA to unwind and separate. The RNA polymerase slides down only one strand of the double stranded DNA and copies it into a strand of mRNA. When the RNA polymerase reaches a special nucleotide sequence of DNA called a "stop signal," the polymerase falls off, the mRNA is released, and the double-stranded DNA winds back into a double helix. After being transcribed, mRNA sections that are not necessary for protein production are trimmed away, and the mRNA is now ready to leave the nucleus and enter the cytoplasm.

Translation

Translation is the process in which a strand of mRNA is used by ribosomes to create a protein. It only takes place in the cell's cytoplasm. First, the nucleotides of the mRNA are organized into sets of three, and each set is called a codon. The codon that spells out AUG (stands for adenine, uracil, and guanine) is called the start codon because it tells a ribosome to assemble there and to begin translation. Once assembled, the ribosome begins sliding down the mRNA, reading each codon and interpreting which amino acid should be added next. **Amino acids** are molecules that

[opposite page] **FIGURE 3.4** During transcription, DNA is copied into messenger RNA (mRNA) in the cell's nucleus. An RNA polymerase enzyme attaches to the promoter signal of the DNA. The double-stranded DNA unwinds and separates as the RNA polymerase copies the DNA into a strand of mRNA. When the stop signal is reached, the polymerase falls off, the mRNA is released, and the double-stranded DNA winds back into a double helix.

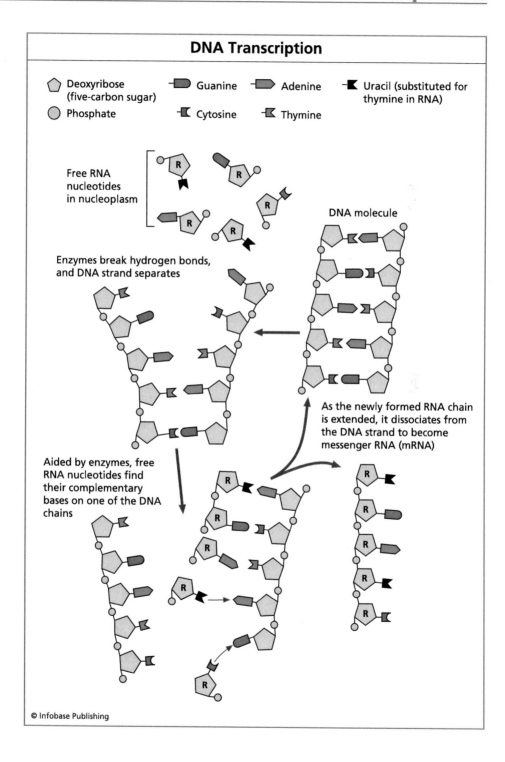

DNA Transcription

Deoxyribose (five-carbon sugar)

Phosphate

Guanine

Cytosine

Adenine

Thymine

Uracil (substituted for thymine in RNA)

Free RNA nucleotides in nucleoplasm

DNA molecule

Enzymes break hydrogen bonds, and DNA strand separates

As the newly formed RNA chain is extended, it dissociates from the DNA strand to become messenger RNA (mRNA)

Aided by enzymes, free RNA nucleotides find their complementary bases on one of the DNA chains form proteins. A special type of RNA, called transfer RNA (tRNA), brings the amino acids to the ribosome. Just as DNA is made up of connecting nucleotides, proteins are made up of connecting amino acids, like beads on a string. Every mRNA codon matches to one of 20 possible amino acids, and because every mRNA begins with AUG, every protein begins with the amino acid called methionine. The ribosome continues sliding along the mRNA and matching the codons to the proper amino acids until it reaches one of three "stop codons" within the mRNA. The stop codons are UAG, UGA, and UAA, and because they do not match any amino acid, the ribosome lets go of the mRNA and the protein is released into the cytoplasm.

Protein shape and function

When the finished protein is released from the ribosome, it is does not float around in the cytoplasm as a straight line. Because each individual amino acid has different chemical properties, when the protein is released from the ribosome, the amino acids begin to interact and form chemical bonds with each other. These interactions result in the protein folding up into a unique three-dimensional shape. Because a certain protein (like factor VIII) has a unique amino-acid sequence, that protein has a unique shape.

The unique shape of each protein determines its ability to perform a specific function. When it comes to proteins, the human body uses something called a "lock and key" mechanism. This means that proteins physically interact with target objects: Some proteins are locks that accept keys, while other proteins are keys that fit into locks. In both cases, if the shape of the protein is altered, then it most likely will not fit properly. This is why the type and size of a gene

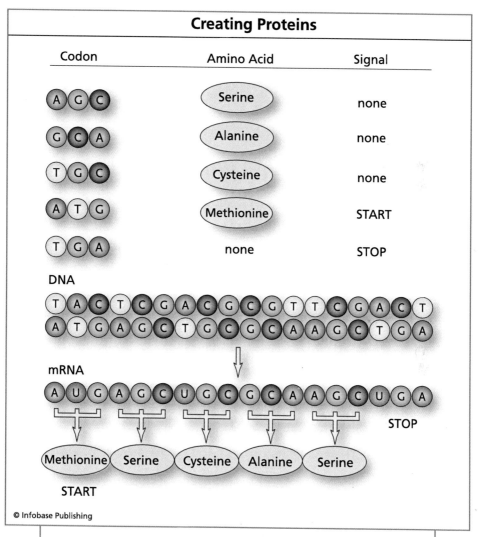

Creating Proteins

Codon	Amino Acid	Signal
A G C	Serine	none
G C A	Alanine	none
T G C	Cysteine	none
A T G	Methionine	START
T G A	none	STOP

DNA

T A C T C G A C G C G T T C G A C T
A T G A G C T G C G C A A G C T G A

mRNA

A U G A G C U G C G C A A G C U G A
                                    STOP

Methionine   Serine   Cysteine   Alanine   Serine

START

FIGURE 3.5 Five codons are shown, four specifying amino acids (protein subunits) and two that serve as start and stop signals. The codons, including the start and stop signals, are linked together to form a gene on the bottom, or coding, DNA strand. The coding strand is copied into messenger RNA (mRNA), which is used to synthesize the protein. Nucleotides appear as round beads: Adenine (A), Thymine (T), Cytosine (C), and Guanine (G). Uracil (U) appears in mRNA.

mutation is important. It all comes down to whether the shape of the protein (in the case of hemophilia, factor VIII or IX) is altered to the point that it can no longer perform its assigned function.

GENETIC MUTATIONS

Hemophilia A is caused by a mutated factor VIII gene, and hemophilia B is caused by a mutated factor IX gene. There are many ways that a mutation can be introduced into DNA. First, before a cell divides to make a new cell, it makes a complete copy of its DNA to put into the new cell. This process is called replication, and considering how many times it occurs each day, it is surprisingly accurate. However, the process of replication is not perfect, and mistakes are made at a rate of one in every 10^{10} (10,000,000,000) nucleotides that are copied. There are specific enzymes whose job it is to find and correct mistakes made during replication, but they sometimes miss a few.

Outside sources can also be the cause of DNA mutations. When a piece of cloth becomes stuck in between the teeth of a zipper, the zipper is no longer able to move. Similarly, chemicals called mutagens can insert themselves into our DNA and prevent the replication enzymes from copying the DNA code correctly. Mutations can also occur if a DNA strand is cut, and chemicals, X-rays, radiation, and sunlight all have the potential to do this. When DNA is cut, the damage may be so large that repair enzymes cannot figure out what the original code was. Because they have to guess when they fill in the missing sections, they may use incorrect nucleotides.

Mutations in the Factor VIII and IX Genes

Not every person with hemophilia A has the same mutation, and the same is true for hemophilia B. In fact, new mutations in the factor VIII and IX genes occur all the time, and although almost every type of mutation has been observed in hemophiliac patients, the most common types of mutations are deletions, insertions, and point mutations. A deletion mutation is when part or all of a gene is missing. Because this type of mutation removes so much information from the gene, a protein cannot usually be made, and the patient will typically experience severe hemophilia. In an insertion mutation, new sections are added to a gene. The effect of an insertion mutation is just as devastating as a deletion. Extra DNA results in extra amino acids, which cause the length and shape of the protein to be incorrect. This extra DNA could also insert a stop codon, causing translation to end prematurely and a nonfunctioning protein to be made.

Another common mutation seen in hemophiliacs is a point mutation. A point mutation involves a change in a single base pair. This change in one nucleotide can still result in an amino-acid change. Whether a person will have hemophilia, and whether it will be severe or mild, depends on the specific amino-acid change. For example, if the amino-acid change created a stop codon, then a short protein would be made, which could result in severe hemophilia. Another example would be if the amino-acid change allowed the protein to be made, but the shape of the protein was altered enough that it could no longer function as an enzyme or a cofactor. These types of changes would prevent the factor VIII or IX protein from being activated during secondary hemostasis. A clotting factor that cannot be activated is of no use, and hemophilia will result.

Inheritance of Genetic Mutations

Both normal and mutated genes are passed from parents to children. This genetic process is called **inheritance**. Although today much is understood about the genetics of inheritance, in the early years of hemophilia this was not true.

Gregor Mendel

The foundation for much of our knowledge of inheritance was laid by a nineteenth-century Czech monk named Gregor Mendel. Mendel was born in 1822 in Moravia, which is in the eastern part of the Czech Republic. At the age of 21, Mendel entered an Augustinian monastery. A monastery is a place were people live to pursue a religious life. In this case, the Augustinians were Roman Catholic men and women who patterned their lives after Saint Augustine of Hippo. These monasteries not only allowed people to pursue spiritual enlightenment, but also encouraged scientific studies as well. Mendel became very interested in the gardens of the monastery and went so far as to attend the University of Vienna, where he studied botany (the study of plants). When Mendel returned to the monastery, he devoted more than 10 years to observing how characteristics are passed from generation to generation in flowering pea plants. He determined that there were specific factors that were inherited. Twentieth-century scientists identified these factors as genes.

Mendel made two important discoveries that are relevant to understanding the inheritance of hemophilia. The first is called the law of segregation. It says that for every genetic trait, a person inherits two forms of the same gene (one from their mother and one from their father). These alternative forms of the same gene are called **alleles**. Mendel also discovered that every allele would be either dominant or recessive. If paired together, the dominant allele will be expressed and the recessive allele will not. This is because the dominant allele is able to silence, or mask, the recessive allele. Dominant genes are indicated by using italicized capital letters and recessive genes are indicated by italicized lowercase letters.

For example, if the allele that codes for the color purple in a plant is the dominant trait, then plants with the alleles

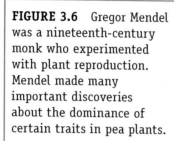

FIGURE 3.6 Gregor Mendel was a nineteenth-century monk who experimented with plant reproduction. Mendel made many important discoveries about the dominance of certain traits in pea plants.

PP and *Pp* will be purple. The *Pp* combination still produces a purple plant because the dominant *P* allele silences the recessive *p* allele, which codes for a white plant. The only way for the recessive color white to be expressed is to have only recessive *pp* alleles and no dominate *P* alleles.

Hemophilia Is a Recessive, X-Linked Disease

Genetic segregation and dominance are important to the disease hemophilia because the mutated forms of the clotting factor VIII and IX genes are recessive and they are both located on the X chromosome. All humans have 23 pairs of chromosomes within each cell. The 23rd pair of chromosomes contains the sex chromosomes and there are two possible types, X and Y. The combination of X and Y chromosomes determine whether a child will be a boy or a girl. Males have the chromosomes XY and females have the chromosomes X X. Because the factor VIII and IX genes are on the X chromosome, the traits of hemophilia and gender are inherited together.

The fact that hemophilia is recessive and X-linked explains why the disease is more common in males. When a man's only X chromosome has a recessive factor VIII or IX gene, the disease hemophilia will be expressed. However, because women have two X chromosomes, when a recessive factor VIII or IX gene is present on one, a dominant gene on the second X chromosome will mask the recessive one and the disease will not be expressed.

WOMEN AND BLEEDING DISORDERS

Hemophilia in a female is very rare, and because it is so rare, girls with any type of bleeding disorder often remain undiagnosed. In other words, many girls do not receive proper treatment for bleeding disorders, because doctors never consider that they might have one.

When a female does have a bleeding disorder, they are often initially misdiagnosed as having a gynecological problem, because one of the first symptoms observed are heavy and prolonged periods. In addition to heavy periods, these girls also experience frequent nosebleeds and prolonged bleeding after dental work. Sometimes these girls are in their mid-20s by the time they are tested for a bleeding disorder.

One of the goals of the National Hemophilia Foundation (NHF) is to heighten public awareness concerning females and bleeding disorders. They are contacting school nurses, because these individuals can be the first to see the symptoms. The NHF is also working to educate gynecologists, pediatricians, and dentists about this problem.

The following chart lists the possible combinations of normal and mutated sex chromosomes and the disease states they generate. The dominant/normal trait concerning hemophilia is designated by a capital *H*, while the recessive/mutated trait is designated as a lowercase *h*.

Genes — **Disease State**

$X^H X^H$ — A normal female

$X^H Y$ — A normal male

$X^H X^h$ — A female that carries the hemophilia mutation but does not experience the disease

$X^h Y$ — A hemophilic male

$X^h X^h$ — A hemophilic female (extremely rare)

To understand how hemophilia is passed down from parents to children, let us examine a series of examples. The first example is a cross between a normal female ($X^H X^H$) and a normal male ($X^H Y$). Because neither of the parents carry a hemophilic mutation, all of the children will be normal.

The next example is a cross between a normal female ($X^H X^H$) and a hemophilic male ($X^h Y$). Because the X chromosome being passed down from the father carries a hemophilic mutation, all of the daughters will be carriers ($X^H X^h$). Because the sons get their X chromosome from their mother, they will be normal ($X^H Y$).

A cross between a carrier female ($X^H X^h$) and a normal male ($X^H Y$) will result in a number of possible offspring. Of the daughters, 50% will be carriers ($X^H X^h$) because they inherited a hemophilic mutation from their mother. Of the sons, 50% will be hemophiliacs ($X^h Y$) because they inherited the hemophilic mutation carried on their mother's X chromosome.

The final example represents a very rare occurrence, the cross between a carrier female ($X^H X^h$) and a hemophilic male ($X^h Y$). Of the daughters, 50% will inherit hemophilic

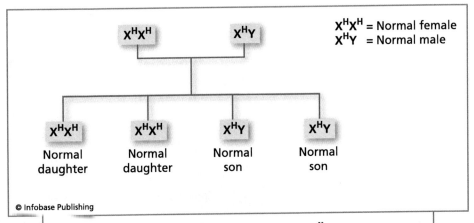

FIGURE 3.7 In the following figures, a black X^H denotes a normal chromosome, while a red X^h denotes a chromosome carrying a mutated factor VIII or IX gene. In this figure, the children of a normal female ($X^H X^H$) and a normal male ($X^H Y$) will all be normal.

mutations from both parents ($X^h X^h$) and will be hemophiliacs; the other 50% will be carriers ($X^H X^h$). Of the sons born to this couple, 50% will be hemophiliacs ($X^h Y$), and the other 50% will be normal ($X^H Y$). This type of match is

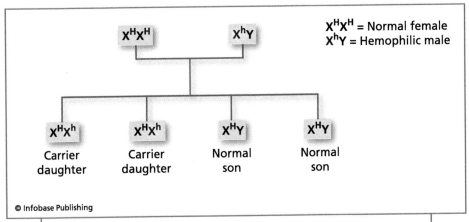

FIGURE 3.8 Of the children produced by a normal female ($X^H X^H$) and a hemophilic male ($X^h Y$), all daughters will be carriers ($X^H X^h$) and all sons will be normal ($X^H Y$).

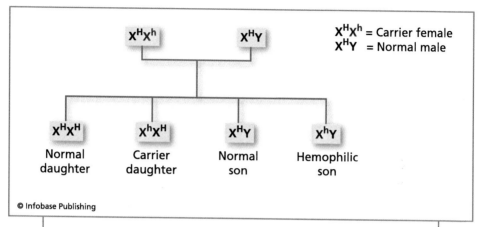

© Infobase Publishing

FIGURE 3.9 Of the children produced by a carrier female ($X^H X^h$) and a normal male ($X^H Y$), for each daughter born there is a 50% probability that she will be a carrier, and for each son born there is a 50% probability that he will have hemophilia.

unusual for the simple fact that hemophilia is a rare disease, so the probability of two people with these genetic traits meeting is unlikely. It is also possible that two people with these traits could decide not to have children.

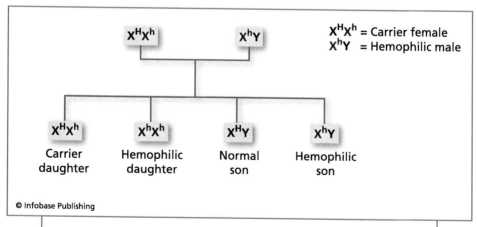

© Infobase Publishing

FIGURE 3.10 Of the children produced by a carrier female ($X^H X^h$) and a hemophilic male ($X^h Y$), all daughters born have an equal probability of being either hemophiliacs or carriers. Sons have an equal probability of being hemophilic or normal.

SYMPTOMS, COMPLICATIONS, AND THE DIAGNOSIS OF HEMOPHILIA

LEVELS OF SEVERITY IN HEMOPHILIA A AND B

The severity of both hemophilia A and B can be described as mild, moderate, or severe. The severity of disease is based on the amount of clotting factor activity in the blood, as compared to a normal blood sample tested at the same time. A patient who has 0% to 1% of normal factor activity has severe hemophilia. About 50% of hemophilia A patients are categorized as severe. Patients who have 1% to 5% of normal factor activity have moderate hemophilia. Patients with 5% to 40% of normal factor activity have mild hemophilia.

The reason that factor activity is measured, and not the amount of factor VIII or IX protein, is because if doctors only measured how much factor VIII or IX was in the blood, they would also be measuring proteins that did not work. This method would give doctors false high values. By measuring factor activity, only the proteins that work are being measured.

DISEASE SYMPTOMS

First, it is important to realize that hemophiliacs don't bleed faster than normal people—they simply cannot stop

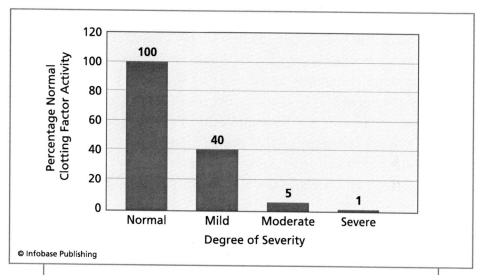

© Infobase Publishing

FIGURE 4.1 The diseases hemophilia A and B are categorized as mild, moderate, or severe based on how well the patient's blood clots. Patients with mild hemophilia have 5% to 40% of normal clotting activity, while a person with 1% to 5% clotting activity is classified as having moderate hemophilia. A person has severe hemophilia when he or she has 1% or less of normal clotting activity.

bleeding. Patients with severe hemophilia are usually diagnosed in the first year of life. They experience heavy bruising and bleeding of the gums as their baby teeth come in, and they suffer unusually severe bruises as they learn to walk. Throughout life, severe hemophiliacs experience spontaneous bleeding episodes, which means that they bleed even though they have not experienced an injury. These spontaneous bleeds occur most often in their joints, but also occur in their muscles and under the skin. Severe hemophiliacs also experience frequent nosebleeds, blood in their urine (from bleeding in their kidneys or the bladder), and blood in their feces (from bleeding in their intestines or stomach).

People with moderate hemophilia usually do not have spontaneous bleeding episodes. Their bleeding problems occur after suffering an injury, even a minor one. In many ways their symptoms are similar to severe hemophiliacs, they just occur less frequently. People with moderate hemophilia are all different when it comes to the disease symptoms they experience, so bleeding episodes can range from once a month to once a year. Because the symptoms of moderate hemophilia are still serious, patients are usually diagnosed before the age of 5 or 6.

Many people with mild hemophilia are not diagnosed until later in life, when they are adolescents or even adults. They do not experience spontaneous bleeding, but without treatment, they can experience prolonged bleeding after major injuries, surgeries, and dental procedures. If someone knows that they have mild hemophilia, they can receive clotting factor prior to surgery or dental procedures to reduce their risk of bleeding. These may be the only times when a person with mild hemophilia receives treatment for his or her disease.

Complications Associated with Hemophilia
Bleeding Into Joints

The majority of all the bleeding episodes that a hemophiliac will experience, whether sporadic or because of trauma, will be joint bleeds. **Hemarthrosis** is the name given to a hemophilic bleeding episode that occurs in the joints. There are many joints in the human body, but 80% of hemarthroses occur in the knees, elbows, and ankles. Only rarely is hemarthrosis observed in the shoulders, hips, hands, and spine.

As a joint bleed begins, patients described an "aura," or a feeling of warmth and tingling as blood begins to flood the joint cavity. The aura may last about two hours. As the bleed progresses, patients often report that they have a feeling of tightness in the joint, but describe the feeling as uncomfortable rather than painful. Unfortunately, as the small joint cavity fills with blood, and the blood presses hard on the nerves within the joint, intense pain follows. At its peak, the joint is severely swollen, hot to the touch, and all movement is lost. The intense pressure of the swollen joint actually helps to slow the bleeding, and once stopped, it will take several days to weeks for the joint to drain and return to normal.

Many hemophiliacs have a joint known as their **target joint**. This joint seems to be one where bleeding occurs most often. Over time, a hemophiliac can develop more than one target joint. For example, in small children, an ankle seems to be a common target joint. At five years and over, the knees and elbows are more frequently the sites of joint bleeds. In adults, the ankles, knees, and elbows are all possible sites of joint bleeds.

Knees are a common target joint in hemophiliacs for two reasons. One, the knees have to support the weight of the body, so they take a lot of stress on a daily basis. Second, the knee joint is made to have a wide range of movement. By being more flexible, the knee joint is also less stable, which makes it more vulnerable to injury. Good muscle strength can help stabilize and protect the knee joints. Unfortunately, when a hemophiliac develops a knee bleed, the knee joint must be kept immobile until the bleeding stops. This results in the muscles around the knee becoming weak from inactivity. Because the muscles that support the knee are weaker after a joint bleed, the joint is now even more susceptible to another bleed. Physical therapy to strengthen the muscles that support the knee can be very helpful in reducing the number of bleeds in that joint.

A target joint usually develops as the result of having experienced several bleeding episodes. Some signs that a

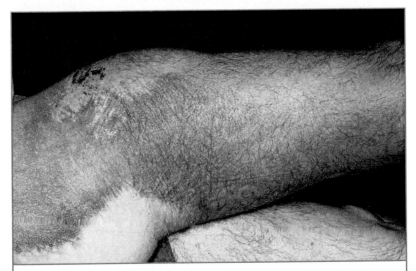

FIGURE 4.2 After experiencing repeated hemophilic bleeding episodes, joints can develop a chronic joint disease called hemophilic arthropathy. The inflammation that occurs during a joint bleed begins to degrade the cartilage. Eventually, the bones have no padding between them, and bone rubbing on bone is very painful.

target joint is developing are continued swelling and warmth after a bleeding episode has ended. What is happening is that the repeated bleeding in the joint irritates the synovial membrane. The synovial membrane is a layer of soft tissue that lines the ends of the bones and secretes cushioning fluid into the joint cavity. When this tissue become irritated, the only defense the body has is to begin a series of reactions that result in inflammation.

Inflammation is actually a complicated set of chemical reactions, but it can be simplified if it is compared to what happens after a very serious crime has been committed. In this case, the irritation to the synovial membrane is the crime scene. The first thing the police would do is shut down all roads that lead away from the crime scene so that the criminals cannot escape and commit more crimes in other places. The body does the same thing; it constricts (tightens) all the blood vessels downstream of the irritation. Next, the police would open up all roads that lead to the crime scene so that the area can fill up with police, ambulances, and other support teams. The body copies this action by dilating (widening) the blood vessels upstream of the irritation. By constricting blood vessels leading away from the irritated area, and dilating blood vessels leading to the irritated area, the irritated area now becomes filled with fluid, blood, and immune cells. All this extra blood and fluid makes the inflamed body part feel hot, look red, and appear swollen. The pain comes from the increased volume of fluid pressing on nerve cells.

After multiple inflammations, the number of cells in the synovial membrane increases, the joint swells up in size and over time starts to look very large and lumpy. The number of blood vessels in the synovial membrane also increases, and more importantly, these blood vessels become very fragile. This is a bad combination for a hemophiliac, because by increasing the number of fragile blood vessels, the joint becomes very vulnerable to bleeding. The result is a target joint that experiences a never-ending cycle of joint hemorrhages, with each bleeding episode making the joint more susceptible to another bleed.

When the target joint developed, it was because the synovial membrane was being constantly irritated by exposure to blood. Over time, repeated bleeding into the joint begins to irritate, and cause inflammation in, the bones and cartilage of the joint. As a result, chronic joint disease, or **hemophilic arthropathy**, develops. Cartilage is a dense tissue that is very similar in structure to the outside of blood vessels. It contains two types of cells: collagen for strength and stability and elastin so that it can be compressed and stretched. Together, these cells make cartilage the perfect padding to go in between bones. Unfortunately, when a joint is experiencing an inflammatory response because of a bleed, it is bombarded with fluids, cells, chemicals, and pressure. Over time, the cartilage can only take so much

NATHAN'S JOINT BLEEDS

Nathan Fatula is a 16-year-old severe hemophiliac who suffers from frequent joint bleeds, sometimes two a week. Because he has had so many, he is very familiar with the warning signs. "First the joint becomes very tight and starts to lose mobility. Then it starts swelling with even more loss of movement, and then it gets really warm, and then there is a lot of pain," he explains. How long the joint bleeds last depend on how aggressively Nathan treats them. "I don't think I've had a bleed I've totally not treated, but say I feel myself bleeding, but I am doing something I don't want to quit and I wait a few hours, that bleed can progress so badly that it might last up to a week. But if I infuse right away, the bleed could pretty much die and never get any worse, or just last a couple of days." In addition to factor infusions, Nathan is also able to make his own splints at home to immobilize the affected joint. "The splinting material is soft and you roll it out and measure how much you are going to need, and then you cut it. You soak the bandage in water and then you mold it behind the joint until it starts to harden, maybe seven minutes." Nathan then explains that after the splint has completely hardened, he holds it in place by wrapping an elastic bandage around the splint and his joint. In spite of his ability to recognize and treat his joint bleeds, unfortunately, Nathan has already begun to show signs of hemophilic arthropathy in one of his elbows.

abuse, and it begins to degrade. When it does, the bones now have no padding between them, and bone rubbing on bone is very painful. This type of condition can occur in people without hemophilia, in which case it is simply called **arthritis**. The term arthritis comes from the Greek words *arthro*, which means joint, and *itis*, which means inflammation. Therefore, hemophilic arthropathy is a form of arthritis that results from chronic bleeding into the joints.

Because joint bleeds can lead to hemophilic arthropathy, it is recommended that joint bleeds be treated at the earliest signs to prevent long-term damage. Clotting factors should be infused promptly, with repeated doses as necessary to ensure complete healing of the joint. Even though it may be hard for them, older children should rest and try very hard to keep the affected joint immobile. There are now home splinting kits available that can make this more convenient. Finally, because strong healthy muscles will help support and protect joints from bleeds, patients should participate in a regular program of muscle stretching and strengthening.

Bleeding in the Brain

The human brain is so important to human life that it must be encased in bone to protect it. The brain is a very complex body organ that is divided into many different parts that perform very specific functions, all of which are necessary for a normal life. This is why **intracranial bleeding** (bleeding inside the brain) is very serious and can be life-threatening. In fact, intracranial bleeding is a leading cause of death in hemophiliacs, with some estimates as high as 25% of all hemopiliac deaths.

Bleeding can occur on the surface of the brain or deep inside. First, the brain is covered in a membrane that contains many blood vessels. When bleeding occurs here, the blood accumulates in the space between the brain tissue and the

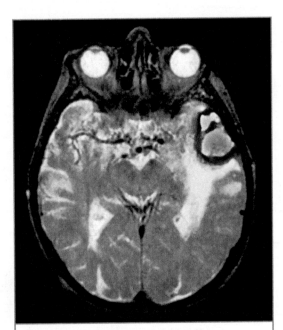

FIGURE 4.3 Intracranial bleeding is bleeding inside the brain. As blood accumulates, it irritates the brain tissue and inflammation results. The bleeding and swelling puts pressure on the many nerves of the brain. Intracranial bleeding is a leading cause of death in hemophiliacs.

membrane that covers it. Second, blood vessels run deep into the inner sections of the brain. When bleeding occurs there, the blood becomes trapped within the brain tissue. Whether bleeding occurs on the surface or deep inside the brain, accumulated blood irritates the brain tissue and inflammation results. The bleeding and inflammation create swelling that puts pressure on the many nerves of the brain. The severity of the bleeding episode determines whether permanent brain damage or death results.

The symptoms of an intracranial bleed can be different depending what part of the brain is bleeding and how much brain tissue is being traumatized. Some of the symptoms of an intracranial bleed include a painful headache that lasts more than four hours, convulsions (violent and uncontrollable contraction of the muscles), double vision, slurred speech, confusion, trouble walking, vomiting, excessive sleepiness, sudden muscle weakness, and intense neck pain. Because an intracranial bleed can easily be life threatening in a hemophiliac, any sign of a brain bleed should be treated immediately.

Inhibitor Antibodies

A problem that many hemophilia patients have to deal with is the development of **inhibitor antibodies**. An antibody is a Y-shaped protein that is produced by an immune system cell called a B cell. Inhibitor antibodies are created in some hemophiliacs because their immune systems begin to see the infused clotting factors as foreign, and therefore a threat. Their bodies respond by producing antibodies that specifically attach to the clotting factors. The antibodies coat the clotting factors and block them from participating in the chemical reactions of secondary hemostasis. The antibodies also act to signal other cells of the immune system that respond by quickly removing the infused factor VIII or IX from the bloodstream. It is not understood why these inhibitors develop, but currently they are observed in 15% to 30% of hemophilia A patients and 2% to 5% of hemophilia B patients. For both hemophilia A and B, inhibitor antibodies are observed more often in people suffering from the severe forms of these diseases. Half of the patients that eventually develop inhibitor antibodies develop them by the age of 10.

Diagnosis of Hemophilia

The diagnosis of hemophilia can be made before birth, in childhood, or later. Different tests are involved, depending on when diagnosis is performed.

Prenatal Diagnosis of Hemophilia

There are two prenatal (before birth) hemophilia tests. In the chorionic villus sampling (CVS) test, a cell sample is taken from the placenta and the factor VIII and IX genes are checked for mutations. The placenta is tissue that develops during pregnancy and lines the pregnant uterus. This test can be performed in the second and third month of a pregnancy.

Amniocentesis is another prenatal test for hemophilia and other disorders. Inside the pregnant uterus is another structure called the amnion, which contains amniotic fluid. It is within the amnion that the baby grows and develops inside the mother. In amniocentesis, a small amount of amniotic fluid is removed, and cells in the fluid are evaluated for mutations in the factor VIII and IX genes. This test can be performed in the fourth month of a pregnancy. Both the CVS and amniocentesis tests have risks associated with them, so they are not performed unless the parents and their doctor decide they are medically necessary.

A mother who suspects that she is a carrier of hemophilia can also undergo two types of testing for hemophilia. She can have genetic tests done, but this requires a sample from a known carrier female in her family to see if they both have matching mutations. The mother's blood can also be tested for levels of factor VIII and IX. While the values from these tests are accurate, they are not reliable measures for whether that mother's child would be a hemophiliac. In fact, carriers of hemophilia A and hemophilia B often have normal levels of factor VIII and IX, respectively.

Diagnosis of Hemophilia in Children and Adults

For a physician to diagnose a child or adult with hemophilia, he or she must first obtain a family history by asking if any other family members have ever had any bleeding problems. Next, even though a diagnosis of hemophilia cannot be made based on clinical symptoms alone, a bleeding history is taken as an important part of the overall medical evaluation. This involves a questionnaire to evaluate whether the patient has experienced excessive or serious bleeding events. Issues of interest to doctors include bleeding into the joints, deep-muscle bruises, bleeding in the brain in the absence of a major trauma, prolonged bleeding after having teeth pulled or being circumcised, blood in the urine or feces, and prolonged or heavy periods in young girls.

The partial thromboplastin time (PTT) and prothrombin time (PT) tests can be done to diagnose a bleeding disorder. The PTT test measures how well the intrinsic and

TESTING NEWBORN BABIES FOR HEMOPHILIA USING CORD BLOOD KITS

The Hemophilia Center of Western Pennsylvania offers a convenient kit to parents with a family history of hemophilia who are expecting a new baby. Even families that choose to give birth at home without a doctor, such as the Amish, have access to these kits. The goal is to find out if the newborn baby has hemophilia without having to draw blood from the baby. Instead, blood from the umbilical cord is collected. The kit contains blood collection tubes with labels and a plastic bag, a lab requisition form that has already been filled out by staff of the hemophilia treatment center, instructions to the doctor delivering the baby on how to collect the sample, and a pre-labeled mailing box. After the doctor has collected blood from the cleaned umbilical cord, the box of samples is mailed on ice to the Coagulation Laboratory at the Institute for Transfusion Medicine (ITxM). The lab measures the levels of clotting factor VIII or IX activity, and a hematologist reviews the lab results and consults with the family. If the testing was inconclusive or not processed correctly, the hematologist notifies the family that further testing is necessary.

common pathways are working, while the PT test evaluates the extrinsic pathway. Each test is performed in a similar manner. First, blood samples are collected into special glass tubes that contain some type of *anticoagulant,* a chemical that will prevent the blood from clotting until it can be tested. Most anticoagulants used in blood collection bind calcium ions, which prevent the reactions of the extrinsic and intrinsic pathways from occurring. When the blood is ready to be tested, ingredients that are necessary for clotting are added, such as calcium, and the samples are then timed to see how long it takes to form a blood clot. Normal values differ depending on the laboratory that is doing the testing, but in general, 25 to 45 seconds is normal for the PTT test and 11 to 15 seconds for the PT test. Prolonged PTT or PT values, such as a PTT time of 90 seconds or a PT time of 50 seconds, are indications of a blood disorder.

The PTT and PT tests only indicate that a patient has a bleeding disorder; they do not tell that the patient has hemophilia or indicate whether it is type A or B. Patients suspected of having a bleeding disorder can undergo a coagulation factor test. These tests evaluate the activity of factors VIII and IX in the patient's blood and determine if they suffer from hemophilia A or B. Factor activity tests can be described using two different values: units and percentage of normal activity. The term "unit" may seem confusing, but all it really means is that one unit is equal to 100% factor VIII or IX activity in 1 milliliter of normal blood. It is important to understand that people without hemophilia do not have consistent factor VIII and IX activity levels in their blood. Instead normal values range from 0.5 unit per milliliter to 2.0 units per milliliter.

Percent activity is the more commonly used value for the coagulation factor tests because it quickly indicates the severity of disease this patient may have. Recall that people with less than 1% activity have severe hemophilia, people with 1% to 5% activity have moderate hemophilia, and people with greater than 5% activity have mild hemophilia (the range of normal percent activity is 50% to 200%). To calculate a patient's percentage of normal activity, the patient's activity in units per milliliter is divided by the activity of a normal blood sample that is tested at the same time. This number is then multiplied by 100%. For example, if the patient's value was 0.01 units per milliliter and the normal sample was 1.0 unit per milliliter, then

$$\left(\frac{0.01}{1.0} \right) \times 100\% = 1.0\% \text{ activity}$$

This person would be diagnosed with severe hemophilia.

5

TREATMENT OF HEMOPHILIA:

Whole-Blood Transfusions to Clotting Factor Concentrates

The evolution of hemophilia treatments started long ago. The first attempt at treating hemophilia may have been as early as the Middle Ages, when the physician Albucasis (discussed in Chapter 2) described cautery as a way to control bleeding in people with bleeding disorders. By the nineteenth century, the most common treatment was simply to advise patients to avoid activities that could lead to injury. In the event of an injury, the treatment methods available were not very advanced. They included cautery, the application of ice, splinting, and even ingesting poisonous substances such as lead, strychnine, and turpentine. Ninety percent of hemophiliacs did not live to see their 21st birthday. This chapter will discuss the treatment of hemophilia with blood transfusions and clotting factors; Chapter 6 will consider treatments that have a genetic basis.

WHOLE-BLOOD TRANSFUSIONS

One of the first breakthroughs in hemophilia treatment came in the form of whole-blood transfusions. This early treatment did not help to stop bleeding episodes. Instead, it replaced some of the blood being lost by the patient.

MEMORIES OF A HEMOPHILIAC

Don Miller almost bled to death when he was circumcised as a baby. His mother and father drove him from Pennsylvania to Johns Hopkins Hospital in Baltimore, where he was diagnosed with severe hemophilia A at 18 months of age. This was a surprise to the Miller family, because there was no history of hemophilia in their family. Don was apparently the victim of a spontaneous mutation. "Most of the time I got no treatment, and when it was life threatening I went to the hospital and got whole blood. When I was young, because the only treatment was for me to go to the hospital, most of the time I just lay at home and suffered. It would take 10 days to two weeks for the bleeding to stop. When I had joint bleeds, my arms were swollen up, or my legs were swollen up. One time, I cut the back of my right knee, I was about seven or eight years old, and it took a month for the seeping to stop. It was not bleeding fast enough to keep me in the hospital and keep giving me blood, so I went home. My parents did not have much money; my dad was a farmer and worked part-time as a sewing machine mechanic. My injury was obviously not life threatening, and so it just seeped blood until the tissues managed to grow back together."

Dr. James Blundell is credited with the first successful person-to-person whole-blood transfusion in 1818. Prior to this, transfusion experiments had concentrated on transferring blood from animals to people, and the majority of those attempts were lethal. Blundell, however, had an emergency. One of his patients was a mother who had just delivered a baby, and because she was hemorrhaging severely, her life hung in the balance. Blundell took a risk and transferred 4 ounces of blood directly from the arm of the woman's

FIGURE 5.1   Dr. James Blundell performed the first successful person-to-person blood transfusion on a young woman by transferring blood directly from her husband's arm into hers.

husband into her arm. The woman lived, and Blundell continued to improve his transfusion techniques and invented some devices for the procedure.

The next achievement is attributed to Dr. Samuel Lane, an English physician, who performed the first successful whole-blood transfusion on a hemophiliac in 1840. The procedure was performed at Saint George's Hospital Medical School in London with the aid of Dr. Blundell. The patient was an 11-year-old hemophilic boy who was bleeding uncontrollably after eye surgery. Lane transferred 12 ounces of blood from a young woman directly into the patient.

Blood Groups

Despite the successes of Blundell and Lane, the science of hematology was still in its infancy, and the transfer of whole blood remained quite risky. This prevented blood transfusion from being widely used as a treatment for bleeding episodes in hemophiliacs. In the early to mid-1900s, two monumental discoveries were made that paved the way for safe blood transfusions. They were the discovery of the ABO blood groups and the Rhesus blood groups.

Everyone has substances on the surface of their red blood cells that are called **antigens**. An antigen is anything that, when introduced into the body, is perceived by a person's immune system to be a threat. If blood from a donor is given to an incompatible recipient, the recipient's immune system attacks the blood and a reaction occurs in which the blood actually clots inside the veins. This type of immune response can be so severe that it can result in the death of the recipient.

There are four blood types based on the four types of antigens that can be present on an individual's red blood cells: AB, A, B, and O. People with type AB blood can receive types AB, A, B, and O blood (they are called "universal receivers"). People with type A blood can receive types A

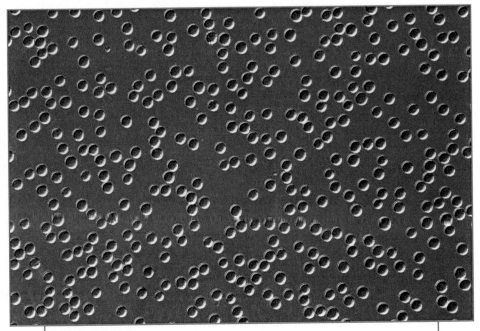

FIGURE 5.2 Normal red blood cells after an infusion of compatible blood.

and O. People with type B blood can receive types B and O. People with type O blood can receive only type O (they are called "universal donors").

The Rhesus factor (Rh D) is another antigen that can be found on red blood cells. The Rh antigen was discovered in 1940 in Rhesus monkeys. If a person has the Rhesus factor, he or she is Rh+ (positive). If he or she does not have the antigen in his or her cells, he or she is Rh− (negative). A person who is Rh+ can receive Rh− blood, but an Rh− person cannot receive Rh+ blood. In summary, the eight possible blood types of the ABO and Rhesus blood groups are AB+, AB−, A+, A−, B+, B−, O+, and O−.

Once blood groups were identified, whole-blood transfusions became safer and were a better treatment option for

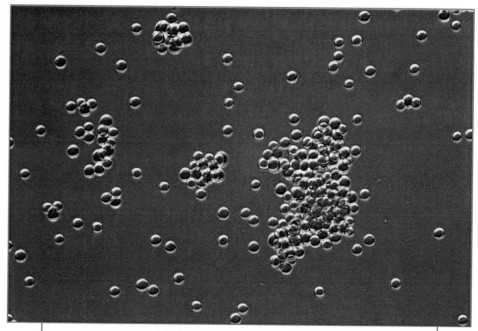

FIGURE 5.3   Clumped red blood cells following a transfusion of incompatible blood. This condition can be deadly, which is why it is important that compatibility be determined before a transfusion.

hemophiliacs suffering a bleeding episode. Whole-blood transfusions were used to treat hemophiliacs into the 1960s, even after new and better treatments were developed. It is important to remember that even after a new and better disease treatment is discovered, it is not always available to everyone. For instance, many people live in remote areas far from the hospitals that can provide new treatments. Perhaps a patient has access to a treatment, but cannot afford it, so they continue to use the older treatments. There is also the possibility that a doctor caring for a hemophiliac in a remote area is not aware of, trained in, or comfortable with a new treatment, and so will not offer it to the patient.

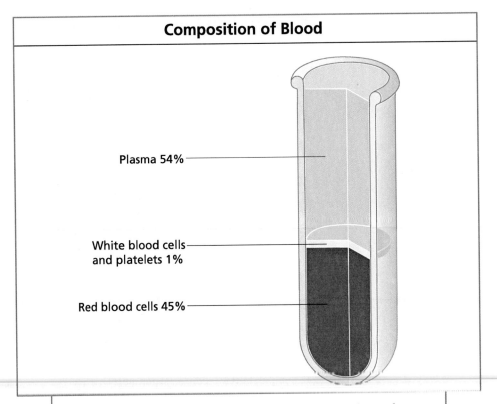

Composition of Blood

Plasma 54%

White blood cells and platelets 1%

Red blood cells 45%

FIGURE 5.4   Blood that has been mixed with an anticoagulant can be separated into two basic parts: liquid plasma and cells. When the blood is allowed to sit, the heavy red blood cells will sink to the bottom, and the slightly lighter white blood cells will be in a layer on top of the red blood cells. The plasma, which contains the clotting factors, remains at the top of the mixture.

Plasma Infusions

The next step in treatment for hemophiliacs involved using only the part of blood that contains the clotting factors. **Plasma** makes up 55% of whole blood and is the liquid portion of blood. To obtain plasma, blood must be collected and promptly mixed with an anticoagulant so that it does not clot. The blood cells are then separated from the liquid plasma either by gravity or by spinning the blood in a machine called a centrifuge. In the early 1930s, Arthur Patek and Richard Stetson found that when plasma was separated from whole blood, it retained the ability to clot blood. Patek and Stetson also found that filtering the plasma to remove any remaining platelet cells did not decrease its clotting activity. These results strongly indicated that whatever elements in the body cause the blood to clot are present in plasma. Next, both of the plasma samples (with and without platelets) were injected into hemophiliacs with positive results. In fact, 150 milliliters of the filtered plasma was able to stop a severe nosebleed in a hemophiliac. This was a great improvement over the use of whole blood.

In 1937, Arthur Patek and another scientist named F. H. L. Taylor were able to remove water from normal plasma, thereby concentrating the clotting factors. Patek and Taylor found that the plasma concentrates were just as effective at clotting blood as whole plasma, but it took a much lower volume of the concentrates to stop a bleeding episode. Being able to use lower volumes was a great convenience to hemophiliacs.

Replacement Therapy

It is important to note that Patek and Stetson made a very important observation during their research. They determined that the defect in hemophilic blood was from the absence of a necessary agent and not the presence of an inhibitory one, and this was evidence for a theory that had existed since the writings in the Talmud. Hemophilia research then centered on identifying what the missing "something" was and replacing it. Once the missing elements were identified in hemophiliacs, in theory, **replacement therapy** for hemophilia seemed simple. Factor VIII would be administered to treat hemophilia A, and factor IX would be administered to treat hemophilia B. In reality, achieving a successful replacement therapy has not been so simple.

Cryoprecipitates

One of the greatest discoveries in replacement therapy for hemophilia was made by Judith Pool at Stanford University in 1964. Pool discovered that when fresh plasma is frozen and then thawed slowly, proteins in the plasma collect in the bottom of the container. These **cryoprecipitates** ("cryo," from the word cryogenic, meaning frozen and "precipitate," meaning a solid substance that has been separated from a liquid solution) were found to contain great quantities of proteins. In spite of the overall high protein concentration of the cryoprecipitates, the amount of clotting factor activity was low, less than one unit per milligram of total protein.

Factor Concentrates

The primary goal in concentrating the clotting factors in cryoprecipitates was to reduce the volume that a severe hemophiliac needed to take to stop a bleed. To review, whole blood is very inefficient at stopping a bleed; it really only replaces the blood that is lost. Scientists continued to make systematic advancements in concentrating clotting factors from blood, which allowed bleeding episodes to be stopped with lower volumes. First, plasma was separated from whole blood, then plasma was concentrated, and next, cryoprecipitates were developed. In spite of these advancements, the volumes being used by severe hemophiliacs, and the frequency of their treatments, remained relatively high. To improve on the situation, researchers worked to concentrate the clotting factors obtained from cryoprecipitates.

The first steps in concentrating cryoprecipitates began in the 1970s, with concentrated factor VIII. The first attempts at concentrating the clotting factors were called **intermediate-purity concentrates**. Cryoprecipitates are a mixture of many different blood proteins, and proteins can have different sizes and shapes, they can be acidic (have a low pH) or basic (have a high pH), and they can have positive (+) or negative (⊠) electrical charges. These characteristics are all determined by the amino acids that make up each protein. In order to concentrate the factor VIII, and later factor IX, scientists studied the shape and chemical characteristics of these proteins and then used chemistry to separate them from the majority of the other blood proteins in the cryo-precipitates. The methods used to separate the factor VIII and IX proteins included temperature changes, pH changes, and the addition of various chemicals like polyethylene glycol and aluminum hydroxide. Compared to the starting cryoprecipitates (activity of less than 1 unit per milligram), the activity of the intermediate-purity concentrates was increased to 10 units per milligram. Although the activity of the intermediate-purity concentrates was 10 times greater than the cryoprecipitates, only 1% of all the proteins present in a sample of intermediate-purity concentrate were factor VIII.

By the 1980's, new treatments for hemophiliacs had been developed, and the life expectancy of people with this disease had increased. Unfortunately, it was then that the hemophilic community was hit hard by two deadly diseases, hepatitis and HIV. The hemophilic community depended on donated blood as its source for clotting factors. As more people became infected with hepatitis and HIV, contaminated blood supplies became more common. Efforts were made to develop quick, easy, and reliable tests to identify contaminated blood. At the same time, scientists hoped that if they could further concentrate the intermediate-purity concentrate clotting factors, they could remove hepatitis and HIV along with unnecessary blood proteins. In the 1980s, **high-purity concentrates** were developed for factor VIII, with factor IX following in the 1990s. To produce high-purity concentrates, several chromatography methods were used. In simple terms, a chromatography procedure separates a mixture into its different parts. For example, ion exchange chromatography separated clotting factor proteins based on their overall electrical charge, and gel filtration chromatography separated them by size. Both ion exchange chromatography and gel filtration did a wonderful job at concentrating the clotting factors, and the average activity of the high-purity factor VIII concentrates rose as high as 50 units per milligram. Unfortunately, although the risk of viral disease was reduced, some HIV and hepatitis viruses remained. Therefore, treatments that would kill the viruses in the concentrates became necessary. First, dry-heat was used, but this was found to be unreliable. Manufacturers of clotting factor concentrates found that using detergents and pasteurization, alone or in combination, was the safest route, and no HIV infections from factor concentrates have been reported since 1986.

In spite of these great advancements, scientists continued to pursue the development of **ultra-high-purity concentrates** by using immunoaffinity chromatography methods. In this type of chromatography, antibodies that recognize the clotting factors are used to grab and pull them away from other proteins. The use of immunoaffinity methods to produce ultra-high-purity concentrates resulted in factor concentrates that were 99% pure, with an activity of 150 units or more per milligram.

Because they are so pure, only a small volume of factor VIII and factor IX high-purity concentrate is needed to stop a bleeding episode. The concentrates are considered safer in terms of disease transmission, and their lower protein content makes them less likely to cause an allergic reaction. Unfortunately, the high-purity concentrates have a drawback. Remember that factor VIII is naturally unstable;

HOW A FACTOR TREATMENT IS GIVEN

Today, many clotting-factor therapies are in a freeze-dried (powder) form, making them easy to store. The clotting factor comes in a sterile glass bottle along with a second glass bottle of sterile water. The tops of both bottles are cleaned with a sterile alcohol pad, and a double-ended needle is used to connect two bottles. One end of the needle punctures the top of the sterile water bottle, and the other end of the needle punctures the top of the bottle containing the clotting-factor powder. Because the clotting-factor bottle has a vacuum, the water is automatically sucked out of its bottle into the bottle containing the clotting factor. After disconnecting the bottles from the needles, the factor bottle is gently rotated to make sure all the powder is dissolved. The less pure the factor, the longer it takes to dissolve. Next, a syringe with a small filter attachment is used to draw up the clotting factor; the filter holds back any particles that did not dissolve. Finally, a small tube that is connected to a very small needle called a "butterfly needle" is attached to the syringe holding the clotting factor. The butterfly needle is used to puncture the vein of the patient and the plunger of the syringe is depressed very slowly. The amount of clotting factor given is determined by the weight of the patient.

it needs the von Willebrand factor (vWF) to hold its three protein sections together. In the ultra-high-purity concentrates, there is no vWF, so it is necessary to add **serum albumin** protein to help stabilize the factor VIII. Serum albumin, which is produced by the liver, is the most abundant protein found in blood. Some people worried that adding another blood-derived protein to the factor VIII concentrates would increase the risk of disease transmission. To date there has been no evidence of this, most likely because the medicine is pasteurized. It is also interesting that some severe hemophiliacs have had more success with the intermediate-purity concentrates, and it is theorized that this could be because of the presence of natural vWF in these preparations.

Other Drugs

There are treatments besides replacement therapy that are used to treat mild hemophilia. For mild hemophilia A, a drug called desmopressin has been shown to be effective. Developed in 1977 and licensed in 1984, desmopressin is a hormone that encourages platelets to stick to an injured blood vessel. The platelets then help increase the concentration of factor VIII. It is given intravenously or as a nasal spray, and has no risk of disease transmission because it is not derived from human blood. Its therapeutic value for hemophilia is limited, though, because it is only effective in people with mild hemophilia A, and not at all effective in people with hemophilia B.

Antifibrinolytic drugs, including tranexamic acid and aminocaproic acid, are other medicines that are used to help keep clots from breaking down. These are also only used for mild hemophilia.

6

TREATMENT OF HEMOPHILIA:

Recombinant Clotting Factors and Gene Therapy

In Chapter 6, we explored the development of treatments of hemophilia that focused on the transfusion of blood or its factors. This chapter will focus on treatments that have a genetic basis, including clotting factors made from recombinant DNA and gene therapy.

RECOMBINANT DNA

Recombinant DNA is created by combining segments of DNA from different organisms. Recombination of DNA takes place naturally in bacteria. In the 1970s and 1980s, scientists developed methods for making recombinant DNA in the laboratory, allowing for the creation of recombinant proteins. For example, a gene that codes for a human protein can be glued into the DNA of a hamster cell. As the cells are grown in the laboratory, they will produce the desired protein. The proteins can be collected, purified, and used as medicines. These methods have been used to produce large quantities of factor VIII and IX for treatment of people with hemophilia A and B.

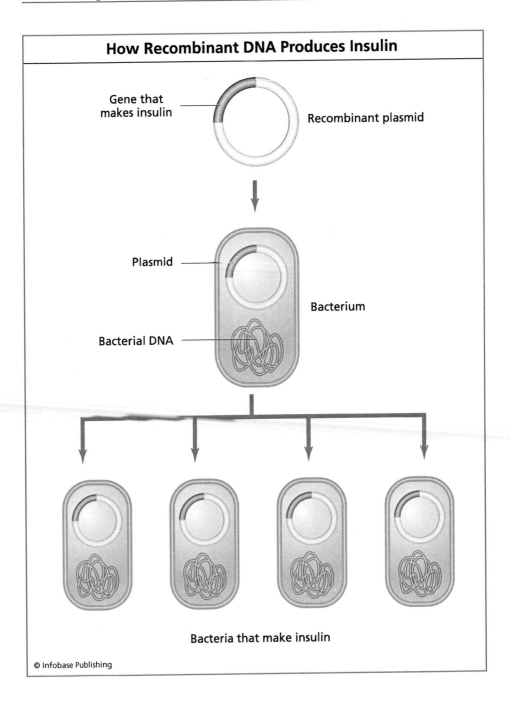

How Recombinant DNA Produces Insulin

Gene that makes insulin

Recombinant plasmid

Plasmid

Bacterium

Bacterial DNA

Bacteria that make insulin

Producing Recombinant Factor VIII and IX

In the 1980s, two separate research groups, at nearly the same time, succeeded at synthesizing the entire factor VIII gene and expressing the recombinant protein. At 186,000 nucleotides long, this was the largest gene ever synthesized at that time, and the recombinant proteins obtained were found to be just as effective at clotting blood as cryoprecipitates. Recombinant factor VIII became commercially available in 1992, and recombinant factor IX followed in 1997. Today, recombinant factor VIII and IX are some of the most commonly used treatments for hemophilia.

To produce a recombinant protein, there are many different and unique molecular biology methods available for use. It is a little like baking a cake; there is a lot of room for individuality. This is also why two separate research teams simultaneously succeeded in producing recombinant factor VIII using different methods. There are, however, basic steps common to producing recombinant proteins, which will be outlined next.

Isolating the Gene to Be Expressed

Before you can produce a recombinant protein, you need a gene, and isolating a human gene can be a little tricky. For hemophilia, the first step was completed in the early 1980s when the genes for factor VIII and IX were isolated and

[opposite page] **FIGURE 6.1** This diagram shows how recombinant DNA technology is used to make medicines such as insulin. Healthy genes that direct insulin production are inserted into a bacterium. The bacterium containing the gene replicates and produces large quantities of insulin. Similar methods are used to produce recombinant factor VIII and IX for hemophiliacs, except that mammalian cells are used instead of bacteria.

sequenced. The factor VIII gene has 186,000 nucleotides, while the factor IX gene has 34,000 nucleotides. In eukaryotic cells, when a gene is transcribed into mRNA, only portions of the transcript actually code for the functional protein, and these sections are called exons. In between the exons are nucleotide sections called introns that do not code for the protein. For example, the factor VIII gene is 186,000 nucleotides long, but only 7,000 of those nucleotides represent exons that code for the functional clotting factor. Why human genes contain introns is still being debated.

Once the gene has been located and its DNA sequence determined, many copies of the gene of interest need to be made. The polymerase chain reaction (PCR) can be used to make billions of copies of a gene within a few hours. In PCR, a region of DNA undergoes DNA replication over and over again. To begin the DNA replication, a primer is needed, which is a short section of DNA that is complementary (so that it can bond to) the section of DNA just before the piece of DNA that is to be copied. Primers supply an available end for the DNA polymerase enzyme to begin adding free nucleotides. In other words, if the gene to be copied were nucleotide numbers 500–900, then you would want to make a primer that attaches to nucleotide numbers 490–499. Just as you have to add a little water "to prime a well," you need a little piece of DNA to get the PCR replication process started.

The PCR fragments are then cut with a restriction enzyme. Restriction enzymes occur naturally in bacterial cells and are a form of protection because they cut up any foreign DNA, such as a virus, that may get inside the cell. Each restriction enzyme is very choosy and cuts at a specific DNA sequence, which are only four to six nucleotides long. Some enzymes make blunt cuts, as if the double-stranded DNA had been cut clean through with a knife. Other restriction enzymes make staggered cuts, where the double-stranded DNA is cut unevenly so that one strand is shorter or longer than the other. The restriction enzymes that make staggered cuts are used a lot in recombinant DNA technology because they generate what is known as "sticky ends," so named because they easily attach onto another piece of DNA cut with the same restriction enzyme.

RECOMBINANT DNA CAME FROM SCIENTIFIC COOPERATION

Dr. Stanley Cohen and Dr. Herbert Boyer attended the same scientific conference in Hawaii in 1972. At the time, Cohen was studying plasmids, which are small round pieces of DNA that are carried inside bacteria and are able to copy themselves independent of the bacterial chromosome. In fact, bacteria pass plasmids around as if they are trading cards, and in the process, are able to pass new genes around in the population. Cohen loved how easy it was to move these plasmids from bacteria to bacteria, even in the laboratory, and he wanted to use them to move specific genes around. In other words, he wanted to use plasmids as "gene buses." By chance, Cohen attended Boyer's lecture on restriction enzymes, the enzymes that can cut DNA in very specific places. Restriction enzymes would enable researchers to cut plasmids and insert DNA into the bacteria. The two scientists ate dinner that night and decided to work together, which was not difficult since their laboratories were only an hour apart in California. Together, the men developed recombinant DNA. Cohen also gave recombinant DNA a special name—chimera, which comes from a mythological beast with a lion's head, a goat's body, and a snake's tail.

Recombinant Protein Expression Vectors

After the gene to be expressed has been isolated, it needs to be put into an **expression vector**. This vector will help transfer the gene of interest into cells that will express that gene's protein. Expression vectors can be made in the lab or purchased out of scientific catalogs. Most expression vectors are circular pieces of double-stranded DNA, and every expression vector needs at least three things: (1) an origin of replication, (2) a gene for antibiotic resistance, and (3) at least one unique restriction enzyme site. The origin of replication allows the vector to copy itself. A gene for antibiotic resistance is necessary because it is difficult to put expression vectors into cells, so it is necessary to be able to separate the cells that took a vector from those that did not. By growing the cells in the presence of an antibiotic, only the cells containing the expression vector and its antibiotic resistance gene will grow. The expression vector must also have at least one unique restriction enzyme site, because the goal is to cut the circular vector only once, insert the gene sequence into the vector, and then glue the pieces together back into a circle. If, for example, the vector had two of the same restriction cutting sites, then the vector would be separated into three separate pieces. This would make it very complicated to reassemble the vector pieces and the inserted gene in the correct order. To put the gene of interest into the expression vector, it is cut once with the same restriction enzyme that was used to cut the PCR copies of the gene. Usually a restriction enzyme that generates sticky ends is used. The PCR copies are then glued into the expression vector using an enzyme called ligase.

Next, the number of expression vectors needs to be increased substantially. To accomplish this, the expression vector is inserted into bacterial cells through a process called transformation. Many cell types, bacterial and mammalian, do not naturally transform; however, simple

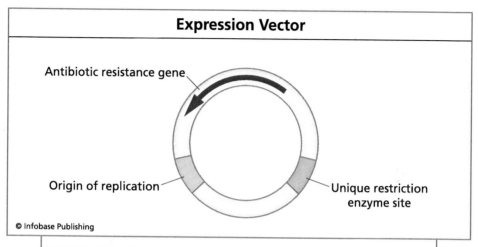

Expression Vector

Antibiotic resistance gene

Origin of replication

Unique restriction
enzyme site

© Infobase Publishing

FIGURE 6.2   Every expression vector needs to contain three
important things: an origin of replication to allow transcription of
the inserted gene; a unique restriction enzyme, so the vector will
be cut only once; and a gene for antibiotic resistance to isolate
the cells that received the vector.

chemical treatments can make the cells cooperate. The
transformed bacteria are grown overnight, and because
they multiply so quickly, a large stock of expression vectors
can be harvested from the cells the next day.

Cell Systems for Expressing Recombinant Proteins

Once a large number of expression vectors have been
obtained, they need to be put into the cells that will express
the proteins. Both bacterial and mammalian cells can be
used to express recombinant proteins. In general, bacterial
cells are less expensive and easier to work with than mammalian cells. If one is attempting to express a mammalian
protein, however, a mammalian cell system may need to be
used. For example, the human clotting factors VIII and IX are
glycosylated, meaning they are coated in sugars by the liver
cells before being released into the blood. These sugars help
protect the proteins and assist in directing them to where

they need to go in the body. Bacteria do not glycosylate proteins. Therefore, to produce the most natural factor proteins possible, a mammalian system is necessary. Both Chinese hamster ovary (CHO) and baby hamster kidney cells can be purchased from scientific suppliers, and both systems have been used to produce recombinant factor VIII. After it is decided whether a mammalian or a bacterial cell system will be used, an expression vector that is compatible with that system must be used. Specifically, the expression vector must contain an origin of replication recognized by that cell system. It also important to grow the host cells in the presence of antibiotic so that any cells that did not receive the expression vector will be killed off. This will allow for easy identification of the recombinant cells.

Purifying the Expressed Protein and Testing That It Is Functional

How the expression vector was constructed and what cell system is used determines whether the expressed proteins are kept inside the cells or secreted into the surrounding cell culture liquid. If the proteins are kept inside, then the cells will need to be broken open. If the proteins are secreted, then the liquid media the cells are grown in has to be collected. Either way, because these proteins are going to be injected into people, it is necessary to make sure they are very pure. Once a pure sample of the expressed protein is obtained, it must then be tested to ensure its concentration and to verify its activity.

Gene Therapy

Gene therapy represents a completely new type of treatment for hemophilia. Gene therapy gets right to the source of a genetic disease by trying to correct the defective gene.

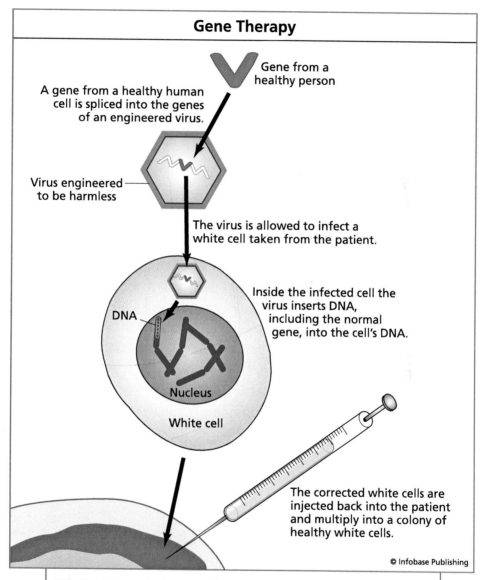

Gene Therapy

Gene from a healthy person

A gene from a healthy human cell is spliced into the genes of an engineered virus.

Virus engineered to be harmless

The virus is allowed to infect a white cell taken from the patient.

DNA

Inside the infected cell the virus inserts DNA, including the normal gene, into the cell's DNA.

Nucleus

White cell

The corrected white cells are injected back into the patient and multiply into a colony of healthy white cells.

© Infobase Publishing

FIGURE 6.3 This diagram shows the ex vivo method of gene therapy. The process begins by inserting a healthy gene into the DNA of a virus. For hemophilia, a normal clotting factor VIII or IX gene is used. In a laboratory, this virus is allowed to infect cells that were collected from the patient. When these corrected cells are reintroduced back into the patient, it is hoped that they will multiply and produce the proteins needed by that patient.

In gene therapy, a functioning gene is transported into the body and cells of a patient. The gene may insert itself into the patient's DNA or it may remain independent; either way, the hope is that the gene will produce the protein that is lacking in the patient, thereby curing the patient of his or her disease. The following sections will cover the details of gene therapy.

How Is Gene Therapy Performed?

The first step in gene therapy is to have a gene to deliver. For hemophilia A and B, this is relatively easy, because the genes for factor VIII and IX have been fully studied. Interestingly, gene therapy researchers have chosen not to deliver the VIII or IX genes in the form in which they exist in the body. Instead, they have pinpointed those sections of the genes that are most necessary for protein production and have made changes to these gene sections using recombinant DNA techniques to increase their transcription and translation efficiency.

The next step in gene therapy is to decide how to deliver the gene into the patient's body; in other words, the gene-therapy vector must be chosen. The most common gene-therapy vectors used today are vectors that are viruses. The biggest benefit of viral vectors is that they naturally invade human cells. It is also because of this natural urge to infect human cells that these vectors must be completely inactivated. This means they must be genetically altered so they cannot cause disease after they are introduced into the patient. The vector also has to be genetically altered to make it harder for the human immune system to recognize it as a dangerous invader, eliminate it, and prevent it from transferring the target gene. In gene therapy for hemophilia, researchers have tested three types of viruses as vectors: retroviruses, adenoviruses, and adeno-associated viruses.

To put the target gene into the viral vector, the viruses are broken open and their genetic material is purified. Next, the viral chromosomes and target gene segments are cut with the same restriction enzyme and the target genes are glued into the viral chromosomes using the ligase enzyme. The recombinant chromosomes are then packaged into new virus particles.

Another point that researchers have to consider is what cells in the body will be targeted by the gene-therapy vector. In choosing a target cell, thought should be given to the natural target of the disease, the lifespan of the cells, how easy the cells are to reach, and how rapidly the cells can multiply. Finally, whether to deliver the vector by in vivo or ex vivo methods needs to be decided. In vivo delivery means that the gene-therapy vector is delivered directly into the patient, by injection either into a vein (IV) or into a muscle (IM). Ex vivo delivery means that a sample of cells is taken from a patient and grown in a laboratory. The target gene is then inserted into the cells; the cells is given time to multiply and then returned to the patient's body.

The early attempts at gene therapy for hemophilia concentrated on an in vivo approach using various viral vectors. In these cases, when the gene-therapy vector was injected into a vein, blood cells were the primary cell targets. When vectors were injected into muscle tissue, muscle cells were the primary cell targets. In comparison, researchers had better success when injecting into muscle tissue. In humans, the liver is the natural site of clotting-factor production, and it would be best to deliver a gene-therapy vector there and have the liver cells express the normal clotting-factor genes. This will necessitate using an ex vivo delivery system, and this is something that scientists are currently working to develop.

The Advantages of Gene Therapy for Hemophilia

Gene therapy is still a new field of medicine. The research necessary to develop a gene-therapy treatment is complicated and expensive. However, the disease hemophilia is an excellent candidate for a successful gene-therapy treatment for two reasons. First, it is a disease where only one gene is at fault. Delivering one gene into a person is more straightforward than if the disease is the result of multiple mutated genes or, worse yet, if entire chromosomes are defective. Second, even if you achieve only a small increase in clotting-factor activity levels, you could improve a patient's situation. For example, an increase in clotting-factor activity of only 1% to 2% could be therapeutic enough to stop spontaneous bleeding episodes.

Not only is it scientifically possible to develop a successful gene-therapy treatment for hemophilia, but this new treatment would be preferable to existing replacement treatments for a number of reasons. First, gene therapy would eliminate any risks associated with using blood-derived clotting-factor products. Many people are still using these products for reasons that range from not having access to other products, not being able to afford the more expensive recombinant clotting factors, or having developed inhibitor antibodies. While the blood supply in developed countries is considered safe from HIV, hepatitis, and other viral diseases, there always remains a small risk. Second, with current replacement treatments, severe hemophiliacs require a great number of treatments, but with gene therapy, it is possible that one treatment is all that a patient would need. Third, with frequent factor treatments comes a very high price tag, so gene therapy could potentially offer a less expensive treatment option. Last, successful gene therapy would eliminate the problem of the development of inhibitor antibodies, which plague so many hemophiliacs today.

Gene-Therapy Trials in Humans

Before any new drug or disease treatment is approved for use in the public, it has to pass four testing stages:

pre-clinical testing and three phases of human trials. Pre-clinical testing is research that is performed on animals to fine-tune the treatment as much as possible to ensure the safety of the first human test subjects. The pre-clinical data is reviewed by the Food and Drug Administration (FDA), and if approved, testing on humans begins. By the 1990s, significant pre-clinical testing for gene therapy in hemophilia had been completed in mouse and dog animal models. It was through this research that scientists tested and evaluated options for gene-therapy treatments in preparation for the first phase (phase 1) of human trials. The results for both factor VIII and IX were encouraging enough that phase 1 human trials were approved by the FDA.

With each phase of human trials the number of volunteers and length of study increase: phase 1 (20–80 volunteers for one year), phase 2 (100–300 volunteers for two years), and phase 3 (1,000 to 3,000 volunteers for three years). The purpose of all three phases of human studies is the same, to evaluate the safety of the treatment and its effectiveness. After the phase 3 trials are over, the research data is reviewed by the FDA, and if approved, the treatment becomes available to the public.

For gene therapy of hemophilia, a number of phase 1 human trials were performed by different research teams. Although the results of these trials were very encouraging in that the vectors were well tolerated by the patients, and that some expression of factor VIII or IX was observed, much more work remains to be done. First, the expression levels achieved were very low, much lower than those seen in animal models. For example, in a study by Dr. Katherine High in Philadelphia, dogs with naturally occurring hemophilia were treated with a viral vector carrying the factor IX gene, and factor levels were increased 12%. None of the phase 1 trials of hemophilia gene therapy in humans saw 12% increases in factor IX levels. Pre-clinical trials are important and necessary, but because humans are unique, the results of animal trials may not accurately predict what will happen in humans. Second, in the phase 1 trials the expression of the factor proteins only lasted a short time, indicating that the immune responses of the human volunteers were disrupting protein expression of the delivered gene. How this was occurring, and how to avoid this problem, remains to be worked out.

Two tragic incidents have caused all human gene-therapy research to significantly slow down and, in some cases, stop altogether. An 18-year-old boy named Jesse Gelsinger had a genetic mutation that caused deadly levels of ammonia to build up in his blood. In September 1999, Jesse was injected with a gene-therapy vector at the University of Pennsylvania's Institute for Human Gene Therapy. Almost immediately after receiving the treatment, Jesse developed a fever, his blood began clotting, his liver hemorrhaged, and his lungs began shutting down. Four days later, Jesse died of multi-organ failure as the result of an intense immune response to the gene-therapy vector. More recently, in 2000, a French research team performed a gene-therapy study on 10 children with a disease called severe combined immunodeficiency disease (SCID). At first, the therapy seemed to be a success, with nine of the 10 children showing great improvements in their health. Unfortunately, several years later, three of the children had developed leukemia, which is a cancer (uncontrolled cell growth) of the bone marrow. It is believed that the virus vector that was used inserted itself into the children's DNA at a place that controls cell growth, thus causing the cancer.

By 2007, so many more regulatory restrictions had been placed on gene-therapy research that many scientists now are frustrated. Dr. Jerry Powell, Professor of Hematology and Oncology, and Director of the Hemophilia Treatment Center at the University of California, Davis says, "There is no such thing as 'no risk' research. If we conduct research, then by definition it means there are unknowns, and therefore, some risk. I think society will need to address this question over the next couple of years, in general, for all biomedical research."

The quest for gene-therapy treatment for hemophilia is continuing, although at a slower pace. Some of the problems that researchers are wrestling with include avoiding triggering the body's immune response so that deaths like Jesse Gelsinger's can be avoided. Avoiding the immune response will also allow the delivered DNA to last longer in the patient, therefore reducing the number of gene-therapy treatments that are needed. Researchers are also looking for alternative delivery vectors and even trying to get away from viral vectors altogether by pursuing ex vivo delivery methods. For those researchers who are still pursuing in vivo delivery methods, much effort is being put into refining the target cells, such as putting the factor VIII and IX genes into the cells of the liver, where the factor proteins are normally produced. This could result in higher expression levels of factor proteins. The most ambitious system would be one in which the delivered gene inserts into the patient's DNA so that it is copied each time the cell divides. This would make one gene-therapy treatment last longer. However, to be successful, there would have to be tight control over where the delivered gene inserts, so that other genes are not destroyed and new diseases such as cancer are not created.

7

LIVING WITH HEMOPHILIA

Hemophilia is a serious disease, and in the past, it greatly restricted a person's lifestyle and often led to an early death. Today, advances in treatment options are allowing hemophiliacs to live longer and fuller lives. Hemophiliacs still have challenges to meet, however, as they find ways to cope with their disease and to lead productive lives.

EDUCATION

The first step in tackling any problem is to learn as much as you can about it. Knowledge is power, so for hemophiliacs and their families, education about the disease is very important. For parents in particular, educating themselves about their children's hemophilia is necessary for them to be able to ensure that their children have the best health care possible. Kerry Fatula, Executive Director of the Western Pennsylvania Chapter of the National Hemophilia Foundation, stresses to parents that "they are their kids' number one advocate, and that they must educate themselves in order to help and protect their children."

The one problem with trying to gather information on any topic in today's high-tech world is that a person may be exposed to as much inaccurate information as they will to good information. Fatula cautions anyone looking for information on hemophilia that "the Internet is a double-edged sword because you can find a tremendous amount of information, but much of it is rife with misinformation. Make sure you are getting information from a reputable source." Anyone seeking information on hemophilia can consult the Internet but then should verify the information gathered by speaking with a physician, someone at a hemophilia treatment center, or someone at one of the various hemophilia foundations. A list of Web sites and sources for further reading are offered at the back of this book.

Doctors

Every hemophiliac needs to be under the care of a physician who is able to manage this type of illness and who has experience in treating hemophiliacs. Physicians with a background in internal medicine and who have further specialized in blood and immune system disorders are the most qualified to treat hemophiliacs. These physicians are commonly called **hematologists**.

Every doctor has had different personal, educational, and professional experiences, with the result that each has his or her own treatment philosophy. Doctors are also human beings, with their own individual personalities. Because hemophilia is a life-long chronic disease, it is extremely important that the patient, and for younger patients, their parents, be happy with their physician. They should never feel intimidated, ignored, or treated in any way that causes them discomfort. Hemophiliacs, and the parents of young hemophiliacs, have to take responsibility for their health, and that starts by choosing a qualified physician who will work productively with the patient to ensure their well-being.

Choice of Treatments

Throughout his or her life, a hemophiliac will continually see his or her doctor for testing and to discuss the best treatment options that are available. As science continues to advance, more and more treatment options become available; therefore, the patient needs to feel that he or she is being fully informed by his or her doctor. For the most part, the selection of hemophilia treatments depends on the severity of the disease, the availability of treatments, and the costs involved. Because the treatment options available today are varied, the decisions that patients will need to make include how to combat inhibitor antibodies, whether to be treated with as-needed or preventative therapies, and whether to be treated at home or at a hemophilia treatment center.

Inhibitor Antibodies

The specifics of inhibitor antibodies in hemophiliacs have been discussed in Chapter 4. In this chapter, their effect on a patient's choice of treatment is discussed. Often, a hemophilia patient is not able to remain on the same type of treatment for their entire life. This may be because better treatment options become available, but it could also be because their current factor treatment stops working. If a patient notices that their present treatment is no longer working, this could be an indication that inhibitor antibodies have developed, and they should see their doctor. Blood tests are available to identify if inhibitors are present in a patient. Next, the amount of inhibitors can be measured using Bethesda units. One Bethesda unit is defined as the amount of inhibitor antibody necessary to inactivate 50% of the factor VIII or IX contained in normal plasma over 2 hours. For example, patients with greater than 5 to 10 Bethesda units per milliliter are called high responders, meaning they have high levels of inhibitor antibodies. More often, a high responder's clotting-factor medicine is blocked by their inhibitor antibodies and they have more difficulty stopping a bleed. Patients with less than 5 Bethesda units per milliliter are categorized as low responders, meaning they have low levels of inhibitor antibodies. Low responders may still experience blocking of their clotting-factor medicine, but to a lesser degree than high responders. Eventually, low responders usually become high responders.

There are a number of strategies for combating inhibitor antibodies. One strategy is to increase the dose of clotting factor to try to overpower the inhibitor antibodies. If this does not work, then immune tolerance therapy (ITT) can be tried. ITT can be performed a number of ways, but the goal is to administer factor VIII or IX every day until the B cells that are producing the inhibitor antibodies become unresponsive. Many studies have been done to test whether high doses or lower doses are more effective at inducing tolerance, and currently, it seems that high doses work better. For example, in North America, the ITT practice is to administer 100 units per kilogram of body weight each day for 420 days. ITT will be successful in about 20% of the people who develop inhibitor antibodies.

In patients with inhibitors in whom ITT has been unsuccessful, switching to a different type of clotting factor is an option. For example, in the last three years, people who have developed inhibitors using recombinant clotting factors have switched to intermediate-purity plasma concentrates with great success. There are several theories as to why intermediate-purity concentrates are a good therapy option. First, in developed countries, there is no longer a significant danger of hepatitis or HIV transmission. Second, these concentrates have the natural attachment of vWF to the factor VIII, and this may help to increase the clotting factor's half-life. Third, it is also possible that the vWF hides the part of the factor VIII protein that generates the inhibitor antibodies. Fourth, because these concentrates are made by human beings, and the proteins are more natural, they may be less likely to be seen as foreign by the patient's immune system. If all else fails, the use of immunosuppressants, drugs that suppress the immune system, could be tried.

As-needed and Preventative Therapies

As-needed therapy simply means to wait until a bleeding episode begins and then administer the appropriate amount of factor. Some hemophiliacs choose preventative therapy, in which factor replacement is given on a constant schedule to try to prevent bleeds from even starting.

The specific schedule for a preventative treatment depends on the severity of the disease. For a severe hemophiliac, infusion of factor may be required every day. Treatments are usually given in the morning, so that a strong level of factor is maintained throughout the day. If an injury occurs, then an extra treatment may be given. The primary advantage of preventative treatments in severe hemophilia in the prevention of hemophilic arthropathy. By preventing bleeds from occurring, damage to the joints is also prevented. The disadvantages of preventative therapy include the greater number of treatments required, the increased difficulty in locating a vein for each treatment, and the increased cost of the clotting factors.

The choice between as-needed and preventative therapy is made between an informed patient and the doctor, and the primary basis for the choice of treatment is the severity of disease. For patients with mild and moderate hemophilia, usually as-needed therapy is recommended with preventative treatments being given in preparation for high-risk activities such as dental surgery. Patients with severe hemophilia more often require preventative treatments.

Some severe hemophiliacs choose the as-needed pathway, however, and accept the increased risk of permanent joint damage.

Home Treatment and Treatment Centers

Both as-needed and preventative hemophilia treatments can be done at home. Home treatments have a number of advantages, including quicker treatment when bleeding occurs, which can mean less damage to joints, and fewer visits to the doctor and/or emergency room, which can save money. Home treatments also allow children and young adults to take responsibility for their own health, which helps them to be independent and develop higher self-esteem. The bottom line is that for severe hemophiliacs that require several treatments each day, home treatment is really a necessity.

Every hemophiliac that takes clotting factor must have it infused (slowly injected) into a vein. For hemophiliacs doing home treatments, finding a vein can be challenging. The type of vein that a patient uses falls into two categories, peripheral and central. Peripheral veins are smaller ones that are located in the arms and the hands. For a hemophiliac to infuse into a peripheral vein, it means inserting a clean needle into the center of the vein. For severe hemophiliacs that require frequent infusions, perhaps several times a day, all these needle sticks can become painful, and even though the needles are small, the constant puncturing of their veins can cause some scar tissue to build up and the overall health of their veins to decrease.

The other option that is available to hemophiliacs is to use one of the central veins, a large vein in the neck, chest, or groin. Typically, the larger veins near the heart are used. To do this, a central venous access device (CVAD) is surgically implanted by a doctor in the patient's chest and can be used for months or possibly years. CVADs can be very convenient for severe hemophiliacs requiring frequent infusions, and in very young children who may fight when someone needs to infuse them. Because this is a surgically implanted device, there is a risk of infection and blood clots, so CVADs need to be regularly checked by a physician.

Many hemophilia treatment centers were established in the United States beginning in 1975. Hemophilia treatment centers are staffed with experts trained in hemophilia treatments. Some of the services usually offered include:

◆ medical treatment
◆ education
◆ counseling and support groups
◆ access to the latest research and clinical trials
◆ instruction on home infusion
◆ genetic testing.

To find the nearest treatment center, a patient should contact the National Hemophilia Foundation or the Centers for Disease Control and Prevention's Division of Blood Disorders.

Coming to Terms with Hemophilia

As with any life-changing medical condition, an individual with hemophilia has to come to terms psychologically with how they will deal with their disease. Some people may choose to deny that they are any different from anyone else. Others may choose to wrap themselves in a blanket of self-pity and allow their disease to rule every aspect of their lives. The best scenario is when patients realize that while they have a disease and may have to expend much energy on maintaining their health, their disease does not have to define who they are as people.

Corey Parker

Corey Parker was 21 years old in 1992 and had just been drafted by the Detroit Tigers minor league baseball team. For Corey, this was the dream of a lifetime, and in his words, "my hemophilia was not going to hold me back." Corey charged into the game that he loved and was determined to take the blows along with the rest of his team. He would not be different; he would not stand out as a hemophiliac. Unfortunately, Corey learned that this way of thinking was just not realistic, although it took him a long time to come to this realization.

For example, two weeks into the season, Corey was hit in the elbow by a pitch, and because he did not know how to self-infuse, getting immediate treatment would mean leaving the game. To Corey, this was not an option, and instead he iced his injury as any other ballplayer would. Other ballplayers' joints would not have bled and swelled to the "size of small watermelon" by the next morning, however. Corey later said that, "I realized that the way that I dealt with my bleeding disorder was holding me back, not the fact that I had hemophilia. It took me a long time to accept the fact that I am different than the other players because of my bleeding condition and, as a result, I need to take better care of myself."

Corey Parker has mild hemophilia, so his ability to absorb a wound with less bleeding is greater than a person who has severe hemophilia. Does that mean that severe hemophiliacs should never do anything that ever puts them in jeopardy of being hurt? How anyone lives their life is really an individual decision, but here is what a few severe hemophiliacs have to say.

Don Miller

Donald Miller is a 58-year-old severe hemophiliac. Don grew up on a farm in Western Pennsylvania where he lived a very active life as a boy. Unfortunately, he says he is now paying for it with aches and pains. Don says that it took him time to learn that, "I can do physical work; I just had to be smart about it. I use levers, tractors, tools, or get someone to help. You have to learn to not do what hurts." Don also learned to recognize when he is experiencing a bleed and to treat it promptly. He does admit that at 58 years old and with arthritis in a number of his joints, it is getting harder to distinguish between the aches and pains of life and a bleeding episode. Because of this, he just has to be more aware of occurrences that could cause bleeding, like falling on the ice, so that if he has pain a day or two later, he knows to give himself a treatment.

Don also believes that reducing the amount of psychological stress in his life has allowed him to deal better with his

SUMMER CAMPS

While hemophiliacs today can live full lives, if they have a severe form of the disease, they do need to exercise caution. Hemophilia summer camps offer a wonderful opportunity for kids to enjoy the "outdoor camp experience" that is so typical of many people's childhoods, while being supervised by staff that are familiar with the disease and trained to deal with bleeding episodes when they occur. These camps also allow hemophiliacs to meet and bond with other kids who are dealing with similar life issues and to gain a sense a community. Many hemophilia summer camps teach children as young as 7 years old how to self-infuse, which only increases their sense of self-confidence, control, and independence. Nearly every state in the U.S. has a hemophilia summer camp, and the National Hemophilia Foundation provides a list.

disease. Many hemophilia researchers agree that the effects of stress on the body can increase the degree and frequency of spontaneous bleeding episodes. In the 1970's, Don made a drastic life decision. He was a young married man attending graduate school in Pittsburgh. He noticed that when he became stressed, because of fighting traffic each day or because of exams, he would experience hemorrhages and end up in the hospital. Don and his wife Barb made the choice of moving to a Pennsylvania farming community where they bought 25 acres of land. Barb got a job at a nearby utility company, and Don stayed home to tend the house, laundry, land, barns, sheep, and horses. Because Don believes that by spending his days in peace, working hard, but having the time to watch the birds, he has been better able to control his stress levels, and therefore, his hemophilia. In fact, Don had also been diagnosed with cirrhosis of the liver in 1979, and was actually told he might only live another three years. After making his lifestyle change, Don's liver regenerated. Don's advice to all hemophiliacs: Don't stress out!

Nathan and Paul Fatula

Nathan Fatula is a 16-year-old boy who was born with severe hemophilia A and who developed inhibitor antibodies at a young age. Nathan is a vibrant, intelligent, and engaging young man who has decided not to let his disease get him down. His hemophilia requires him to receive frequent infusions of clotting factor; in fact, "there have been many times when I have had to treat every six hours." Nathan handles this all with maturity. The frequency of his treatments was also a reason why Nathan decided to attend a Cyber Charter school. The school nurse at his public school was not comfortable with either him or her administering his factor infusions, and going home for each treatment was just not an option. Nathan still remains socially active and feels that he is more productive and healthy by pursuing his education at home.

When Nathan was in 7th grade, he still attended public school. When asked whether he participated in gym, he answered that he only sat out when he already had a bleed or the activity was a "for sure" for bleeding, such as wrestling. Even at a young age, Nathan had learned to recognize his limitations, but this did not mean it stopped him from participating in life. "Dodge ball, that was actually fun. Now

HEMOPHILIACS TAKE PERSONAL RESPONSIBILITY FOR THEIR HEALTH

Hemophiliacs do not have the luxury of being careless with their health. Taking care of their bodies is a large part of everyday life, and they need to be more aware of their environment than people who do not have bleeding disorders. For example, hemophiliacs have to learn to avoid the many over-the-counter products that contain anticoagulation ingredients. The most common of these are aspirin and a group of drugs called nonsteroidal anti-inflammatory drugs (NSAIDs), including ibuprofen and naproxen. These medications drastically interfere with the clumping of platelets and are very dangerous to severe hemophiliacs.

When an injury does occur, hemophiliacs need to stop and ask, "What is the potential for this to result in a serious bleeding episode?" If ever in doubt, a patient or parent should call their doctor or a hemophilia treatment center. Many times, hemophiliacs will experience minor injuries that will require the same first aid treatment used by people without a bleeding disorder. For cuts or abrasions, the injury should be washed with soap and water, first-aid cream applied, and

and then, I would get a bleed, but it was worth it. You can't let hemophilia stop you from having fun."

Nathan has an older brother, Paul, who is also a severe type A hemophiliac. While Paul is more reserved than Nathan is, he too handles his disease with honesty and maturity. Hemophilia is an unpleasant fact for these young men, but neither has allowed it to define who they are as people. When asked what they would tell other hemophiliacs, both boys responded, "Do what you want to do. Don't let the hemophilia

a clean bandage placed over the cut. Next, the injury should be treated with R.I.C.E; this means rest, ice, compression, and elevation.

1. Rest: Stopping all activity will allow the blood pressure to drop, which will help reduce the flow of blood.
2. Ice: Apply cold to the injury for 15 to 20 minutes. Reducing the temperature of the injured area encourages the constriction of blood vessels and helps slow bleeding. Ice can burn the skin, so when applying ice, it should be wrapped in fabric and monitored constantly.
3. Compression: Gentle pressure applied to the injured area for 5 to 10 minutes will help to constrict blood vessels and slow the flow of blood. Care must be taken not to apply too much pressure, which could result in a second bleeding event.
4. Elevation: If possible, raise the site of injury above the heart to reduce the flow of blood.

stop you from everything. There is a ton of stuff you can still do even though you have hemophilia." Nathan added, "I'm not saying, go be a WWE wrestler . . . well, unless you really want to, but just have fun, do what makes you happy."

A Normal Life?

Because of today's advanced treatments, most hemophiliacs live relatively long lives. The question is, do they live "normal" lives? Many people, when asked that question, may respond, "How do you define normal?" Do hemophiliacs have to do things differently than people without bleeding disorders? The answer is *yes*. Do hemophiliacs live worse lives than people without bleeding disorders? That depends on the individual attitude of the person.

GLOSSARY

Allele Different forms of the same gene. One allele is donated by the father and one by the mother.

Amino acids The building blocks of a protein. There are 20 naturally occurring amino acids, each having unique chemical properties.

Antigens Any substance that causes the body to mount an immune response.

Arthritis A medical condition that results in the joints becoming swollen and painful.

Autosomal chromosomes Any of the 44 chromosomes that are not sex chromosomes.

Chromosome Condensed threads of genetic material, composed of DNA and proteins, found inside the nucleus of a cell just before cell division. Human cells have 46 chromosomes.

Clotting factors Blood proteins that are necessary for blood to clot and are missing in hemophiliacs.

Coagulation A change from a liquid to a thick or hardened state. As blood clots it coagulates.

Cryoprecipitates The substance that collects at the bottom of a container when frozen plasma is slowly thawed. It is rich in clotting factors. Discovered by Judith Pool in 1964.

DNA (deoxyribonucleic acid) The molecule responsible for hereditary that is constructed of chains of nucleotides, exists in the shape of a double helix, and is localized in the cell's nucleus.

Enzymes Proteins that drive a specific chemical reaction.

Expression vector A small, circular piece of DNA that is inserted into a particular host for the purpose of producing a protein.

Factor IX A protein produced from a gene located on the X chromosome. Factor IX is a protease enzyme that participates in the intrinsic pathway of secondary hemostasis and is missing in people with hemophilia type B.

Factor VIII A protein produced from a gene located on the X chromosome. Factor VIII is a cofactor that circulates in the bloodstream with von Willebrand factor, participates in the intrinsic pathway of secondary hemostasis, and is missing in people with hemophilia type A.

Fibrin Clot The goal of secondary hemostasis. Results when fibrin molecules have been woven in and around a platelet plug (the product of primary hemostasis).

Gene Specific section of DNA that codes for a specific protein product. Genes are handed down from parents to children.

Gene therapy A method for treating genetic diseases where a mutated gene is repaired or replaced with a working gene.

Hemarthrosis A medical term that describes bleeding into a joint.

Hematologist A doctor who specializes in treating people with blood disorders.

Hemophilia An inherited bleeding disorder that is mostly observed in males. There are two types, hemophilia type A and type B.

Hemophilia type A A recessive X-linked bleeding disorder that results in a lack of clotting factor VIII.

Hemophilia type B A recessive X-linked bleeding disorder that results in a lack of clotting factor IX.

Hemophilic arthropathy Arthritis that results from repeated bleeding into a joint.

Hemostasis The processes by which the body stops bleeding.

Hepatitis C Inflammation of the liver caused by the hepatitis C virus.

Hepatitis C virus (HCV) A single-stranded RNA virus that is transmitted by body fluids and results in the life-long disease of hepatitis C.

High-purity concentrates Factor VIII and IX preparations that are concentrated from cryoprecipitates using ion exchange chromatography or gel filtration chromatography. The preparations are more pure than intermediate-purity concentrates.

Human immunodeficiency virus (HIV) A retrovirus that infects and destroys T cells of the human immune system, causing the disease called *AIDS*.

Immunoaffinity purification Methods that use antibodies to isolate a single type of protein from a complex mixture.

Inheritance The passing of genetic traits from parents to children.

Inhibitor antibodies Antibodies produced by hemophiliacs that block the ability of infused factor VIII or IX to stop bleeding episodes.

Intermediate-purity concentrates Factor VIII and IX preparations that are concentrated from cryoprecipitates using methods that separate proteins by size, shape, or electrical charge. These preparations are less pure than high-purity concentrates.

Intracranial bleeding Bleeding inside the brain.

Mutation   A change in the nucleotide sequence of a gene. Mutations can be inherited from a parent along with their genes, or they can spontaneously occur.

Nucleotides   The building blocks of DNA. Each nucleotide is made of a phosphate, a sugar, and a nitrogenous base. Depending on the nitrogenous base, there are four kinds of nucleotides: A, T, C, and G.

Plasma   The liquid part of blood that still contains the clotting proteins.

Platelet pluq   The goal of primary hemostasis. A mass of activated platelets that work to temporarily plug a hole in a blood vessel.

Platelets   Small blood cells that do not have a nucleus and are important in blood clotting.

Recombinant DNA   The DNA that is formed by combining segments of DNA from different organisms.

Replacement therapy   Any treatment protocol for hemophilia where formulations of clotting factor are given.

Ribonucleic acid (RNA)   A molecule constructed of chains of nucleotides where each nucleotide contains the sugar ribose. RNA is found in the cell's nucleus and cytoplasm and facilitates DNA replication. There are various forms of RNA including messenger RNA (mRNA) and transfer RNA (tRNA).

Serum albumin   A common protein found in blood that is often used to stabilize recombinant or ultra-high-purity concentrates of clotting factor VIII.

Sex chromosomes   The two chromosomes that are not autosomal and determine the sex of a organism. Two X chromosomes result in a female. A male results from an X and a Y chromosome.

Spontaneous mutation   A mutation that suddenly appears in a person instead of that person having inherited it.

Target joint   A joint in a hemophiliac that experiences frequent bleeding episodes.

Transcription   The process by which a DNA strand is copied into a strand of messenger RNA (mRNA).

Translation   The process by which a strand of mRNA is used by ribosomes to produce a protein.

Ultra-high-purity concentrates   Factor VIII and IX preparations that are concentrated from cryoprecipitates using antibodies. These preparations are more pure than high-purity concentrates.

von Willebrand factor (vWF)   A blood protein that is found attached to collagen fibers on the outside of blood vessels that helps to activate platelet cells. This protein also circulates in the blood associated with factor VIII and helps to stabilize the three protein sections of factor VIII.

BIBLIOGRAPHY

Antonarakis, S.E. "Molecular Genetics of Coagulation Factor VIII Gene and Haemophilia A." *Haemophilia* 4, Suppl. 2 (1998): 1–11.

Applegate, Edith J. *The Anatomy and Physiology Learning System*, Philadelphia: W.B. Saunders Company, 1995.

Aronova-Tiuntseva, Yelena, and Clyde Herreid. "Hemophilia: "The Royal Disease," The National Center for Case Study Teaching in Science Web site. Available online. URL: http://www.sciencecases.org/hemo/hemo.asp. Accessed January 25, 2007.

Carlson, Chad. "General Information on Hemostasis," Hematology Resource Page, University of Illinois-Urbana/Champaign Carle Cancer Center Web site. Available online. URL: http://www.med.uiuc.edu/hematology/PtClotInfo.htm. Updated on June 26, 2001.

"Coagulation Factor IX," Haematologic Technologies Inc. Web site. Available online. URL: http://www.haemtech.com/Zymogens/Factor_IX.htm. Accessed January 2007.

Colowick, A. and others. "Immune Tolerance Induction In Hemophilia Patients With Inhibitors: Costly Can Be Cheaper." *Blood* 96 (2000): 1698–1702.

DiMichele D., and E.J. Neufeld. "Hemophilia: A New Approach to an Old Disease." *Hematology/Oncology Clinics Of North America* 12 (1998): 1315–1344.

Everything You Need to Know about Diseases. Springhouse, Pa.: Springhouse Corp., 1996.

Fatula, Kerry. Executive Director of the Western Pennsylvania Chapter of the National Hemophilia Foundation. Interviewed by author. Tape recording. Pittsburgh, Pa., February 28, 2007.

Fatula, Nathan. Interviewed by author. Tape recording. Ellwood City, Pa., March 22, 2007.

Fatula, Paul. Interviewed by author. Tape recording. Ellwood City, Pa., March 22, 2007.

The Gale Encyclopedia of Genetic Disorders. Detroit: Gale Group, 2002.

"The History of Hemophilia," The Canadian Hemophilia Web site. Available online. URL: http://www.hemophilia.ca/en/2.1.2.php. Accessed February 14, 2007.

Hoffman, Ronald, and others. *Hematology, Basic Principles and Practice*, 2nd ed. New York: Churchill Livingstone, 1995.

"How Is Hemophilia Treated," National Heart, Lung & Blood Institute, National Institutes of Health, Department of Health and Human Services Web site. Available online. URL: http://www.nhlbi.nih.gov/health/dci/Diseases/hemophilia/hemophilia_treatments.html. Updated in March 2006.

"In Their Own Words, NIH Researchers Recall the Early Years Of AIDS: January 29 and February 8, 1993 interview with Harvey Klein," Office of NIH History Web site. Available online. URL: http://www.history.nih.gov/NIHInOwnWords/docs/klein1_03.html. Accessed January 12, 2007.

Johnson, M., and A. Thompson. "Hemophilia A," Gene Reviews, University of Washington Web site. Available online. URL: http://www.geneclinics.org/profiles/hemo-a/details.html. Updated August 17, 2005.

Kaufman, Randal. "Advances Toward Gene Therapy for Hemophilia at the Millennium." *Human Gene Therapy* 10 (1999): 2091–2107.

Kavakli, K., and L.M. Aledort. "Circumcision and Haemophilia: A Perspective." *Haemophilia* 4 (1998): 1–3.

Kimball, John. "Blood Clotting," Kimball's Biology Pages Web Site. Available online. URL: http://users.rcn.com/jkimball. ma.ultranet/BiologyPages/C/Clotting.html. Updated on January 1, 2007.

Manno, C., and others. "AAV-Mediated Factor IX Gene Transfer To Skeletal Muscle In Patients With Severe Hemophilia B." *Blood* 101 (2003): 2963–2972.

Mannucci, P.M. "AIDS, Hepatitis and Hemophilia in the 1980s: Memoirs From an Insider." *Journal of Thrombosis and Haemostasis* 1 (2003): 2065–2069.

Matsui, William. "Hemophilia A," MedlinePlus Medical Encyclopedia Web site. Available online. URL: http://www.nlm. nih.gov/medlineplus/ency/article/000538.htm. Updated on May 3, 2006.

Mehta, Satyen. "The Classic Cascade," Department of Internal Medicine, College of Medicine, University of Florida Web site. Available online. URL: http://medinfo.ufl.edu/year2/ coag/classic.html. Accessed November 2007.

Miller, Donald N. Interviewed by author. Tape recording. Mount Pleasant, Pa., March 8, 2007.

Otto, John C. "An Account of an Hemorrhagic Disposition Existing in Certain Families." Reprinted from *The Medical Repository* 6 (1803): 1–4.

Parker, Corey. "Lessons I Have Learned," The Hemophilia Foundation of Southern California Web site. Available online. URL: http://www.hemosocal.org/stories_main.html#. Accessed on April 11, 2007.

Powell, Jerry. Director of the Hemophilia Treatment Center at the University of California, Davis. Email conversation with author, April 22, 2007.

Powell, J., and others. "Phase 1 Trial of FVIII Gene Transfer for Severe Hemophilia A Using a Retroviral Construct Administered by Peripheral Intravenous Infusion." *Blood* 102 (2003): 2038–2045.

Ragni, Margaret. Director of the Hemophilia Center of Western Pennsylvania. Interviewed by author. Pittsburgh, Pa., January 15, 2007.

Professional Guide to Diseases, 8th ed. Philadelphia: Lippincott Williams & Wilkins, 2005.

Rodriguez-Merchán, E.C. "Effects of Hemophilia on Articulations of Children and Adults." *Cinical Orthopaedics and Related Research* 328 (1996): 7–13.

Rosendaal, F.R., and others. "Hemophilia Treatment in Historical Perspective: A Review of Medical and Social Developments." *Annals of Hematology* 62 (1991): 5–15.

Snustad, D.P., M.J. Simmons, and J.B. Jenkins. *Principles of Genetics*. New York: John Wiley & Sons, 1997.

Standish, Diane. Hemophilia Center of Western Pennsylvania. Email conversation with author, March 22, 2007.

Thompson, Arthur. "Structure, Function, and Molecular Defects of Factor IX." *Blood* 67 (1986) 565–572.

"Too Much Bleeding: The Perils of Hemophilia." *Blood: Bearer of Life and Death*. Chevy Chase, Md: Howard Hughes Medical Institute, 1993.

Tuddenham, E.G.D. and M. Laffan. "Purified Factor VIII." *British Medical Journal* 311 (1995): 465–466.

"Von Willebrand Factor," Haematologic Technologies Inc. Web site. Available online. URL: http://www.haemtech.com/Cofactors/vWF.htm. Accessed January 2007.

"What Are the Signs and Symptoms of Hemophilia," National Heart, Lung & Blood Institute, National Institutes of Health, Department of Health and Human Services Web site.

Available online. URL: http://www.nhlbi.nih.gov/health/dci/ Diseases/hemophilia/hemophilia_signs.html. Updated in March 2006.

Wirt, Daniel. "The 1902 Examination Paper on Principles and Practice of Medicine," John P. McGovern Historical Collections and Research Center, Houston Academy of Medicine, Texas Medical Center Library Web site. Available online. URL: http://mcgovern.library.tmc.edu/data/www/html/ people/osler/1902Exam/Question%2022b.htm. Updated on March 8, 2006.

FURTHER READING

Brynie, Faith Hickman. *101 Questions About Blood and Circulation: With Answers Straight From the Heart.* Brookfield, Conn.: 21st Century, 2001.

Brynie, Faith Hickman. *Genetics And Human Health.* Brookfield, Conn.: Millbrook Press, 1995.

Espejo, Roman. *Gene Therapy.* San Diego: Greenhaven Press, 2004.

Freedman, Jeri. *Hemophilia.* New York: Rosen Publishing Group, 2007.

George, Linda. *Science on the Edge—Gene Therapy.* San Diego: Blackbirch Press, 2003.

Kelley, Laureen A. *My Blood Doesn't Have Muscles!: How Children Understand Hemophilia From Preschool to Adolescence.* Centeon Educational Materials, 1996.

Naff, Clay Farris. *Exploring Science and Medical Discoveries— Gene Therapy.* Detroit: Greenhaven Press, 2005.

Rabin, Staton. *The Curse of the Romanovs.* New York: Margaret K. McElderry Books, 2007.

Sheen, Barbara, and Beverly Britton. *Diseases and Disorders— Hemophilia.* San Diego: Lucent Books, 2003.

Willett, Edward. *Hemophilia.* Berkeley Heights, N.J.: Enslow Publishers, 2001.

Yount, Lisa. *Great Medical Discoveries—Gene Therapy.* San Diego: Lucent Books, 2002.

WEB SITES

American Society of Clinical Hypnosis
http://www.asch.net/genpubinfo.htm
American Society of Clinical Hypnosis is the largest U.S. organization for health and mental health care professionals using clinical hypnosis.

The Canadian Hemophilia Society
http://www.hemophilia.ca/en/index.html
The Canadian Hemophilia Society is an organization that works to assist all people with inherited bleeding disorders including hemophilia, von Willebrand disease, rare factor deficiencies, and platelet disorders.

Department of Health and Human Services, Centers for Disease Control and Prevention, Division of Blood Disorders
http://www.cdc.gov/ncbddd/hbd/default.htm
The Centers for Disease Control and Prevention (CDC) is a part of the U.S. Department of Health and Human Services, which is the primary Federal government agency dedicated to improving public health in the United States and globally. The CDC's Division of Blood Disorders works to assist people with certain hereditary blood disorders.

EMedicine From *WebMD- Hemophilia*
http://www.emedicine.com/med/topic3528.htm
eMedicine was launched in 1996, and is one of the largest and most current clinical knowledge bases available on the internet.

National Center for Biotechnology Information— Hemophilia A
http://www.ncbi.nlm.nih.gov/books/bv.fcgi?rid=gnd.section.95&ref=sidebar

NCBI was established in 1988 as a national resource for molecular biology information. NCBI offers a number of literature databases, which include textbooks on health and disease.

The National Hemophilia Foundation

http://www.hemophilia.org

The National Hemophilia Foundation is a United States organization dedicated to finding better treatments and cures for bleeding and clotting disorders. The NHF also works to advance education, advocacy, and research concerning these diseases.

U.S. National Library of Medicine, MedlinePlus—Gene Therapy

http://www.nlm.nih.gov/medlineplus/genesandgenetherapy.html

As part of efforts to offer information to the public, the National Institutes of Health (NIH) supports the website MedlinePlus, which offers information on health topics and drugs, in addition to a medical encyclopedia and dictionary.

ThereforYou.com

http://www.thereforyou.com

Thereforeyou.com, previously called Hemophilia Galaxy, is an informational website offered by the Baxter pharmaceutical company. The site offers general information on hemophilia, treatments, and community programs.

The World Federation of Hemophilia

http://www.wfh.org/index.asp?lang=EN

The WFH is an international, not-for profit organization that works to improve standards of treatment, promote advocacy, provide education, and advance medical research concerning hemophilia.

For a list of hemophilia treatment centers:

The National Hemophilia Foundation at 800–42-HANDI or handi@hemophilia.org

Department of Health and Human Services, Centers for Disease Control and Prevention, Division of Blood Disorders, Hemophilia Treatment Centers
http://www.cdc.gov/ncbddd/hbd/htc_list.htm

For a list of hemophilia summer camps:

The National Hemophilia Foundation—Summer Camp Directory
http://www.hemophilia.org *(In search bar, type summer camp directory.)*

PICTURE CREDITS

INDEX

A

ABO blood groups, 73–74
Account of an Hemorrhagic Disposition Existing in Certain Families, An (Otto), 27
adults, diagnosis in, 66–69
AIDS, 39
Albucasis, 26–27, 70
Alexandra, Czarina, 32–35
alleles, 50
Al-Tasrif (Albucasis), 27
American family study, 27–29
amino acids, 44, 46
aminocaproic acid, 82
amniocentesis, 66
ancient descriptions, 25–27
ancient remedies, 70
animal trials, 95–96
antibodies, inhibitor, 65, 94, 100–102
antifibrinolytic drugs, 82
antigens, 73
arteries, 18
arthritis, 63
arthropathy, hemophilic, 61–63
as-needed therapy, 102–103
aspirin, 108
autosomal chromosomes, 14
autosomal inheritance, bleeding disorders and, 23–24

B

babies, hemophilia testing kit for, 67
bacterial flora of intestine, vitamin K production by, 15
Bethesda units, 100
Biggs, Rosemary, 9
bleeding disorders
    factor XI deficiency, 23
    von Willebrand disease (vWD), 23–24
    in women, 52
bleeding episodes
    brain bleeding, 63–65
    causes of, 56–58
    joint bleeding, 58–63
    stress and, 106–107
blood clotting, components required for, 16–17
blood, donated, virus contamination of, 35–39
blood groups, 73–74
blood transfusions, 70–75
blood vessels, in primary hemostasis, 17–18
blood-borne viral infections, 35–39
Blundell, James, 71–73
Boyer, Herbert, 87
brain, bleeding in, 63–65
British royal family, 29–32

C

calcium, in coagulation, 17, 22
carriers, women as, 14, 66
cautery, 27, 70

cell systems for expressing recombinant proteins, 89–90

cells, prokaryotic vs. eukaryotic, 40

central venous access device (CVAD), 103–104

children, diagnosis in, 66–69

chimera, 87

chorionic villus sampling (CVS), 65–66

Christmas disease, 9. *See also* hemophilia B

Christmas, Steven, 9

chromatography, 80

chromosomes, 12–14

circumcision, 26, 71

clinical trials, gene-therapy, 94–97

clotting factors. *See* factors, clotting

coagulation, components required for, 16–17

coagulation factor tests, 68–69

codons, 44, 46

cofactors, 21

Cohen, Stanley, 87

common pathway, 19, 22

complications

    brain bleeding, 63–65

    inhibitor antibodies, 65, 94, 100–102

    joint bleeding, 58–63

contact actuation (intrinsic) pathway, 19, 20–22

cryoprecipitates, 78

CVAD (central venous access device), 103–104

CVS (chorionic villus sampling), 65–66

D

deletion mutation, 49

deoxyribonucleic acid (DNA), 11, 40–41

desmopressin, 82

diagnosis

    in children and adults, 66–69

    in newborn babies, 67

    prenatal, 65–66

    in women, 52

DNA (deoxyribonucleic acid), 11, 40–41

doctor selection, 99

dominant traits, 50–51

double helix, 40

E

education about hemophilia, 98–99

endothelium, in initiation of hemostasis, 18

English royal family, 29–32

enzymes, 20

eukaryotic cells, 40

exons, 86

expression vectors, 88–89

extrinsic (tissue factor) pathway, 19

F

factor activity tests, 68–69

factor VIII, 10, 22

factor VIII gene, 48–49, 86

factor IX, 10, 11, 21, 22

factor IX gene, 48–49, 86

factor XI deficiency, 23

factor concentrates, 78–82

factor replacement therapy, 77–82

factors, clotting
　activation of, 21
　described, 10–11
　infusions of, 81, 103–104
　recombinant. *See*
　　recombinant clotting
　　factors
　roman numeral
　　designations for, 19
family study, first, 27–29
Fatula, Kerry, 98–99
Fatula, Nathan, 62, 107–109
Fatula, Paul, 109–110
fibrin clot, 19
first aid treatment, 108–109

G

Gelsinger, Jesse, 96
gene isolation, 85–87
gene therapy
　advantages of, 93–94
　human trials in, 94–97
　objectives of, 90–92
　procedure for, 92–93
genes
　DNA and, 11
　dominant vs. recessive,
　　50–51
　hemophilia mutations and,
　　48–49, 86
　size of, and number of
　　mutations, 12
gene-therapy vectors, 92–93, 97
genetic mutations. *See*
　mutations
German royal family, 32

H

HCV (hepatitis C virus), 35
hemarthrosis, 58–63

hematologists, 99
hemophilia. *See also specific
　topics, e.g.,* treatment
　coping with. *See* living
　　with hemophilia
　description of, 7, 9
　severity levels of, 56
　types of, 9–10
hemophilia A, 9–11
hemophilia B, 9–10, 11
hemophilia C (factor XI
　deficiency), 23
hemophilia treatment centers,
　104
hemophilic arthropathy, 61–63
hemostasis
　blood clotting in, 16–17
　defined, 15
　primary, 17–18
　secondary, 19–22
hepatitis C epidemic, 35–37, 79
hepatitis C virus (HCV), 35
High, Katherine, 95
high responders, 100–101
high-purity concentrates, 79–80
history of hemophilia
　Albucasis on, 26–27
　ancient remedies, 70
　in British royal family,
　　29–32
　development of modern
　　treatments, 70–73, 76–78
　in European royal
　　families, 32
　family study in America,
　　27–29
　hepatitis and HIV
　　epidemics, 35–39
　in Russian royal family,
　　32–35

Talmudic writings on, 25–26
HIV (human immunodeficiency virus), 38–39, 79
home treatment, 103–104
Hopff, Frederick, 29
human immunodeficiency virus (HIV), 38–39, 79
human trials, gene therapy, 94–97
hypnosis, 34

I

ibuprofen, 108
immune tolerance therapy (ITT), 101
immunoaffinity purification methods, 37, 80
inflammation, 60–61
information sources, 98–99
infusions, technique for, 81, 103–104
inheritance of hemophilia, 11–12, 51–55
inheritance of mutations, 49, 51–55
inhibitor antibodies, 65, 94, 100–102
insertion mutation, 49
intermediate-purity concentrates, 78–79, 101–102
intestinal bacterial flora, vitamin K production by, 15
intracranial bleeding, 63–65
intrinsic (contact actuation) pathway, 19, 20–22
introns, 86
ITT (immune tolerance therapy), 101

J

joints, bleeding into, 58–63

K

knee joint bleeds, 59

L

Lane, Samuel, 73–74
law of segregation, 50
Leopold, Prince, 29, 31–32
liver, clotting factor production by, 16, 37
living with hemophilia
doctor selection, 99
education, 98–99
personal stories, 104–110
summer camps, 106
treatment choices, 99–104
"lock and key" mechanism, 46
low responders, 101

M

men, hemophilia prevalence in, 14
Mendel, Gregor, 50–51
messenger RNA (mRNA), 42
Method of Medicine, The (Albucasis), 27
Miller, Don, 71, 105–107
mRNA (messenger RNA), 42
mutagens, 48
mutations
causes of, 48
deletion, 49
in factors VIII and IX genes, 48–49, 86
frequency of, and gene size, 12
inheritance of, 49, 51–55
insertion, 49

mutations *(continued)*
    point, 49
    role in disease
        occurrence, 12
    spontaneous, 14

N

naproxen, 108
National Hemophilia
    Foundation (NHF), 52
Nikolai Romanov II, Czar, 32–35
nonsteroidal anti-inflammatory
    drugs (NSAIDs), 108
nucleotides, 12, 40–41

O

Otto, John C., 27
over-the-counter products with
    anticoagulant properties, 108

P

pain relief, hypnosis and, 34
parents, as advocates, 98–99
Parker, Cory, 105
partial thromboplastin time
    (PTT), 67–68
Patek, Arthur, 77
Pavlosky, Alfredo, 9
PCR (polymerase chain
    reaction), 86
peripheral veins, 103
personal stories of
    hemophiliacs, 62, 71, 104–110
physician selection, 99
plasma, 76
plasma infusions, 76–77
plasmids, 87
platelet plug, 18
platelets, 16, 18
point mutation, 49

polymerase chain reaction
    (PCR), 86
Pool, Judith, 78
Powell, Jerry, 96–97
pre-clinical testing, 95
prenatal diagnosis, 65–66
prevalence of hemophilia, 9, 14
preventative therapy, 102–103
primary hemostasis, 17–18
primer, 86
prokaryotic cells, 40
proteins
    production of, 11–12,
        41–46
    shape and function of,
        46–48
prothrombin time (PT), 67–68
PT (prothrombin time), 67–68
PTT (partial thromboplastin
    time), 67–68

R

Rasputin, 33–37
recessive traits
    described, 50–51
    hemophilia as, 51–52
recombinant clotting factors
    cell systems, 89–90
    development of, 85
    expression vectors, 88–89
    gene isolation, 85–87
    purification and testing, 90
recombinant DNA, 83, 87
recombinant protein expression
    vectors, 88–89
replacement therapy, 77–82
replication, 48
restriction enzymes, 86–87
retroviruses, 39
Rh D (Rhesus factor), 74

Rhesus factor (Rh D), 74
ribonucleic acid (RNA), 35
R.I.C.E., 109
RNA polymerase, 44
RNA (ribonucleic acid), 35
RNA viruses, 35, 38–39
royal families, hemophilia in,
    29–35
Russian royal family, 32–35

S
Schönlein, Johann Lukas, 29
SCID (severe combined
    immunodeficiency), 96
secondary hemostasis, 19–22
    common pathway, 19, 22
    extrinsic pathway, 19
    intrinsic pathway, 19,
        20–22
serum albumin, 81
severe combined
    immunodeficiency (SCID), 96
severity levels, 56
sex chromosomes, 14, 51–55
sex-linked traits, 14, 51–52
Spanish royal family, 32
spontaneous bleeding
    episodes, 57
spontaneous mutations, 14
Stetson, Richard, 77
stress, and bleeding episodes,
    106–107
summer camps, 106
symptoms, 56–58. See also
    complications
synovial membrane, 60, 61

T
Talmud, 25–26
target cells, 93

target joint, 59–60
Taylor, F. H. L., 77
tenase complex, 22
testing for hemophilia. See
    diagnosis
tissue factor (extrinsic)
    pathway, 19
tranexamic acid, 82
transcription, 12, 41–44
transfer RNA (tRNA), 46
transfusions
    hepatitis C and HIV
        epidemics and, 35–39
    whole blood, as treatment,
        70–75
translation, 12, 44–46
treatment. See also gene
    therapy; recombinant
    clotting factors
    administration of factor
        concentrates, 81,
        103–104
    ancient remedies, 70
    antifibrinolytic drugs, 82
    desmopressin, 82
    factor replacement
        therapy, 77–82
    infusion technique, 81,
        103–104
    options for, 100–104
    plasma infusions, 76–77
    whole blood transfusions,
        70–75
treatment centers, 104
tRNA (transfer RNA), 46

U
ultra-high-purity concentrates,
    80–81
umbilical cord testing, 67

V

vectors
  expression, 88–89
  gene-therapy, 92–93,
    96–97
veins
  defined, 18
  infusions into, 81,
    103–104
Victoria, Queen, 29–32
viral vectors, for gene therapy,
  92–93
virus inactivation methods,
  37, 80
virus replication, 35, 38–39
viruses
  blood product
    transmission of, 35–39
  hepatitis C virus, 35
  human immunodeficiency
    virus, 38–39, 79
  retroviruses, 39
  RNA viruses, 35, 38–39
vitamin K, 14–15, 17

von Willebrand disease (vWD),
  23–24
von Willebrand, Erik Adolf, 23
von Willebrand factor (vWF),
  11, 18, 22, 81, 82, 101
vWD (von Willebrand disease),
  23–24
vWF. *See* von Willebrand factor

W

whole blood transfusions,
  70–75
women
  bleeding disorders in, 52
  as carriers, 14, 66
  hemophilia prevalence
    in, 14

X

X chromosomes, 14
X-linked disease, 14, 51–52

Y

Y chromosomes, 14

ABOUT THE AUTHOR

Michelle Raabe, Ph.D., holds a degree in molecular virology and microbiology from the University of Pittsburgh School of Medicine. The medical research projects that she has worked on range from babies infected with HIV to vaccine development for horses. As a teacher, she has taught college classes in microbiology, human biology, and anatomy and physiology. Raabe has published in a number of science journals and is currently working as a science writer and developmental editor.